MUSEUM BUILDERS IN THE WEST: THE STANFORDS AS COLLECTORS AND PATRONS OF ART

/

Museum Builders in the est

The Stanfords
as Collectors and
Patrons of Art
1870–1906

by Carol M. Osborne

with essays by
Paul Venable Turner and
Anita Ventura Mozley

and a note by
Mary Lou Zimmerman Munn

Stanford University Museum of Art
Stanford University
1986

This publication has been made possible
by a generous grant from
The National Endowment for the Humanities

This is the twentieth in a series of books
published by the Department of Art,
Stanford University. Lorenz Eitner, Chairman

Library of Congress Catalog Card Number: 85–63383

Cover: Carolus-Duran, Leland Stanford Junior,
1881 (detail of standing figure. See p. 46.)
PHOTOGRAPH BY LEO HOLUB

Contents

    CAROL M. OSBORNE
    Associate Director and Curator of Collections
    Stanford University Museum of Art

    PAUL VENABLE TURNER
    Professor of Architectural History
    Stanford University Department of Art

    ANITA VENTURA MOZLEY
    Curator of Photography
    Stanford University Museum of Art

    MARY LOU ZIMMERMAN MUNN
    Curatorial Assistant in Classical Archaeology
    Stanford University Museum of Art

Acknowledgments

MUSEUM PROJECTS inevitably involve the contributions of many people, and for this history of the Stanford Collection in its early years, colleagues and friends at the University and elsewhere are to be thanked—for scholarly information, thoughtful advice, and practical know-how. A generous grant from the National Endowment for the Humanities has made possible not only this publication but also the permanent exhibition, in the Stanford University Museum of Art, of the Stanford Family gallery, a miscellany of portraits and memorabilia.

At the Museum, I am particularly grateful to Anita Mozley, curator of photography, for her contributions to this exhibition and to Patrick Maveety, curator of Asian art, for many conversations about Leland and Jane Stanford as art patrons and collectors. I owe much to our curatorial colleagues in anthropology and classical archaeology—to Bert Gerow, Priscilla Murray, Mary Lou Zimmerman Munn, and Isabelle Raubitschek—for the cataloguing of objects mentioned in the text. Early on, Betsy Fryberger, curator of prints and drawings, read part of the manuscript, and her comments were a useful guide to its final form. To a succession of Museum registrars—to Susan Roberts-Manganelli and, before her, Nancy Bavor and Kate Kimelman—I extend gratitude for countless details as well as for the taking of many of the photographs included in this account. The Museum's technical staff—Jeff Fairbairn, Frank Kommer, and Larry Lippold—is to be thanked for the skillful installation of the permanent exhibition, as is Marty Drickey, the Museum's administrator, for the careful preparation of wall labels. JoAnne Paradise helped me design the display. For assistance with research, I am indebted to Leslie Flint and Katie Solomonson, and for proofreading, to John Ziemer. Frank Murray was invaluable at the word processor.

I should also like to thank Roxanne Nilan and Linda Long for cordial briefings and patient searches in the Stanford University Archives, and for providing still other photographs of the years before 1906.

In the Stanford Art Department, John LaPlante was kind enough to describe the Museum's situation during the nearly forty years of his association with the University. Paul Turner's work on the architecture of the campus has been immensely helpful in shaping an impression of Leland Stanford as designer and patron.

Joseph Baird, Jr., generously lent us his copious notes on the Big Four as collectors in addition to providing other sources of information about the history of art in California. For scholarly opinions about specific objects in the Collection, I should like to thank Bernard von Bothmer, Masatomo Kawaii, Christine Lilyquist, Charles von Siclen, and Melinda Takeuchi. Nicolai Cikovsky, Jr., obliged us by giving the manuscript a critical reading and I am indebted to him for his helpful comments, as I am to Jean McIntosh for acting as consulting editor. Comments and suggestions contributed by other friends and colleagues have been acknowledged, where possible, in the endnotes.

I want especially to thank Ann Rosener for the gifts of time, friendship, wit, and candor that went into the making of this book, the latest of the many publications she has designed for the Stanford Museum. My greatest debt is to the Museum's director, Lorenz Eitner, who, against the odds, began the resuscitation of the Museum when he came to Stanford as chairman of the Art Department in 1963. Although he has his own view of the founders and their art collection, he has by now made their museum a vital part of our university's life and history.

Carol M. Osborne
Stanford University Museum of Art

Illustrations

9

10

Chronology

1824
Birth of Leland Stanford near Troy, New York, on March 9, son of an innkeeper. After attending Cazenovia Seminary, he was apprenticed to an Albany law firm and admitted to the New York bar in 1848.

1828
Birth of Jane Lathrop in Albany, on August 25, daughter of a prosperous merchant. She attended Albany Female Academy for a year and a half.

Josiah Stanford, Leland Stanford's father (artist unknown).

1850
Marriage of Leland and Jane in Albany, September 30.

1852
Leland Stanford goes west to California to join his brothers and opens a store in Eldorado County. In New York Jane cares for her father until his death.

1855
Jane Stanford joins her husband in California. They move to Sacramento the following year.

1861
Formation of the Central Pacific Railroad in Sacramento by the Big Four, Stanford as president. He is elected governor of California.

1868
Birth of Leland Stanford Junior on May 14.

1869
Completion of the transcontinental railroad celebrated by the driving of the Last Spike on May 10.

Leland Stanford's boyhood home, from the painting by Thomas Kirby Van Zandt.

1874
After nineteen years in Sacramento, the Stanfords move to San Francisco.

1876
Purchase of the Palo Alto estate and the establishment of the Palo Alto Stock Farm.

1878–79
Stanford/Muybridge serial motion photographs in Palo Alto.

Dyer Lathrop, Jane Stanford's father, oil on canvas by Thomas Kirby Van Zandt.

1880–81
First trip to Europe. Acquisition of family portraits in Paris, sculptures in Rome, and Old Master paintings in Florence.

1883–84
Second trip to Europe.

1884
Death of Leland Stanford Junior in Florence on March 13. The Stanfords resolve to found a university and museum in his memory.

1885
Founding grant of the Leland Stanford Junior University, dated November 11. Stanford elected to serve as U.S. senator from California.

1891
Opening of the University.

1893
Death of Leland Stanford on June 21.

1894
Opening of the Leland Stanford Junior Museum.

1905
Death of Jane Stanford on February 28.

1906
The San Francisco earthquake, April 18.

The Lathrop family home, oil on canvas by Thomas Kirby Van Zandt.

Leland Stanford, 1848

Jane Stanford, 1850

1871

1874

1882

*1 The Leland Stanford Junior
Museum in 1905, a year before
the San Francisco earthquake
destroyed three-quarters of the
building. The central pavilion
now houses the Stanford
University Museum of Art.*

Introduction

'. . . the grandest museum in the world'

2 *The Metropolitan Museum of Art in Central Park at the turn of the century. The Fifth Avenue building, designed by Richard Morris Hunt, was not completed until 1910.*

Tʜᴇ ᴍᴜsᴇᴜᴍ of Art at Stanford University is unique among American museums for having been founded by a private family as a general collection of world art on a par, in the 1880s, with the great public museums being built at that time. Among these were the Metropolitan Museum of Art in New York and the Boston Museum of Fine Arts, both founded in 1870 by groups of art-minded citizens. By the turn of the century, however, the Stanford Museum was housed in a structure larger than either of these city museums; indeed, it was the largest privately owned museum building in the world (1,2,3). Opened to visitors in 1894, its archaeological and ethnological holdings were a rarity on the Pacific Coast; by 1905, its collection of Far Eastern materials was unsurpassed in the western United States.[1] But perhaps more startling than the Museum's phenomenal growth was its sudden collapse: in 1906, the San Francisco earthquake leveled three-quarters of the huge structure and symbolically set into motion years of decline. Revitalized since the 1960s in concert with the art history program at Stanford, the Museum's encyclopedic beginnings have long been forgotten despite their singularity. This book attempts to reconstruct the Museum's original make-up —both the architectural achievement it represents and its broad holdings—as well as to study the art patronage of its founders in the context of the American Renaissance.

Like the University, the Leland Stanford Junior Museum was founded by the railroad millionaire Leland Stanford and his wife, Jane, as a memorial to their only child, a gifted boy who died at fifteen of typhoid fever while traveling abroad with his parents. Leland Stanford Junior (1868–1884) had been seriously interested in collecting art and in studying classical archaeology, interests his parents fostered in significant ways. When he was twelve, he was taken to Pompeii, Vesuvius, and Rome by his mother, who encouraged him as they traveled to collect

3 *The Museum of Fine Arts, Boston, designed by John H. Sturgis, in 1876.*

mementos of the sites he had seen. During the following winter, which the family spent in New York, his father became a patron of the Metropolitan Museum of Art, and Leland studied its archaeological collections with his tutor, becoming well acquainted with the Metropolitan's director, Luigi Palma di Cesnola, excavator of the antiquities of Cyprus. During this period, Leland seems to have conceived the idea of becoming involved, as Cesnola later recalled, in "the art-training of our American people."[2] In any case, when the youth set out for his second trip abroad, he carried with him Cesnola's letter

5 *Roman blown-glass urn, first or second century* A.D. (SM 10955)

8 *Egyptian bronze cat, Twenty-sixth Dynasty.* (SM 17260)

7 *Palmyrene sepulchral relief, second century* A.D. (SM 17200)

16

4 *Egyptian Middle Kingdom relief fragment from the tomb of Intef at Abydos.* (SM 17202)

6 *Attic red-figure bell krater, c. 430* B.C., *by the Polygnotos Group.* (SM 17411)

of introduction to Sir Philip Cunliffe Owens,[3] director of the South Kensington Museum, later renamed the Victoria and Albert. With its emphasis on popular education, the British institution was in many ways the model for the modern American museum. It was one of dozens of English and Continental museums visited by the three Stanfords in their travels as they gradually worked their way south to the National Museum in Athens.

In Paris in the fall of the year, Leland spent many hours at the Louvre, where he became conversant, in particular, with Egyptian archaeology (4).[4] Encouraged by his father, who gave him money to spend on the little museum he had started at home, the boy went about with his tutor acquiring Egyptian bronzes, Greek vases, Roman sculpture, glass, ancient coins, and the like from the best dealers in Paris, Athens, and Rome (5–8). Finally,

on a visit to Greece, only months before his death, Leland's pursuits were given encouragement by the most celebrated archaeologist of the age, Heinrich Schliemann, the Homeric scholar, linguist, and pioneer excavator who shortly before had rediscovered in Anatolia the site of ancient Troy. Schliemann's achievements were a source of controversy and fascination at this time and they prompted the Stanfords to think of an archaeological museum as an appropriate way to perpetuate the memory of their talented son.

Nonetheless, it is of interest to note that the idea of supporting a public collection had long been in Governor Stanford's mind. The stimulus seems to have come, at least partially, from a visit paid to Sacramento in 1872 by the famous naturalist Louis Agassiz. Years later, David Starr Jordan, first president of Stanford University and a natural scientist by training, recalled with pleasure "the admiration, almost veneration, of both Mr. and Mrs. Stanford for the educational ideals and personality of Agassiz," Jordan's teacher, who had once been the Stanfords' guest.[5] Stanford was one of a group of prominent citizens who subsequently founded the Agassiz Institute for the promotion of interest in the arts and sciences.[6] (Judge E. B. Crocker was to serve as curator of the fine arts division.) Having moved from Sacramento to San Francisco in 1874, Stanford redirected his philanthropy to his new home, and in 1882 he bought with

Charles Crocker a natural-history collection that would become, the newspapers noted, the nucleus of a British Museum for the city of San Francisco. The Ward Collection of geology, natural history, and mineralogy, purchased for $16,000, was given by the two men to the California Academy of Sciences. The donors spoke of it "as an encouragement to wealthy Californians to contribute to a school of research for the rising generation and a practical college of art information at the disposal of scientists."[7]

Although the Stanfords included museums and galleries of art in the memorial University's founding grant of November 11, 1885, they spoke two years later of locating the museum building in Golden Gate Park as a gift to the people of San Francisco. According to news reports, they were determined to do what their son would have done had he lived—"leave to San Francisco the grandest museum in the world."[8] Indeed, they announced that they were making it their purpose to add to Leland's collection, so that "it shall form a great repository of curious and instructive objects, comparing favorably with the most famous of European museums." Mrs. Stanford was anxious to begin work on the project so that "within her lifetime she might see the accomplishment of her son's design in the completion of a monument which, more than any of the other splendid memorials for the perpetuation of his memory," would express the specific nature of his intelligence and taste. Ultimately, the Stanfords chose the Palo Alto campus as its site, and in 1892, when the building was nearing completion, a story appeared in the *New York Times* telling that it was Mrs. Stanford's wish that "a large portion of her husband's great fortune be devoted to building up and maintaining the museum" so that it might serve not only Stanford students but also college students elsewhere on the West Coast.[9] Characteristically American was her view that a museum should serve an educational purpose.

By 1893, the year of Governor Stanford's death, Mrs. Stanford had added fifteen thousand articles to her son's modest beginnings. This prodigious feat was accomplished by the resolute buying up of collection after collection, all in conformity with intentions Leland Stanford Junior had expressed during his lifetime, namely, adding continually to the nucleus of Egyptian, Greek, and Roman objects, and beginning a collection of Chinese and Japanese curiosities as well as relics of the American mound builders.[10] Indeed, within months of their son's death in 1884, the Stanfords had opened negotiations with the Metropolitan Museum for the acquisition of five thousand duplicates from the Cesnola collection of Cyp-

riot antiquities.[11] The next year, Mrs. Stanford bought from the New Orleans Exposition of 1884–85 the William McAdam collection of American mound relics, a rare collection that spans the entire prehistoric era of the Midwest. In Washington in 1888, the Stanfords acquired the DeLong collection of Japanese objects, to be followed in 1892 with the acceptance of a collection formed by Eugene M. Van Reed, Queen Victoria's consul general to Japan from 1866 to 1873 that included an album of 187 *surimono* prints.[12] Abroad in 1888, Jane Stanford purchased a collection of Greek antiquities formed by a classical scholar, Athanasios Rhousopoulos.[13] By the early 1890s, the John Daggett collection of Northwest Coast Indian material was in place and the Stanfords had accepted from their young friend Timothy Hopkins a large collection of Korean objects gathered by a Methodist missionary, Henry G. Appenzeller.[14] Also from Hopkins had come, in 1893, a sizable collection of Coptic textiles assembled by the famous British Egyptologist Sir William Flinders Petrie.[15] Soon after, Hopkins joined Petrie's Egypt Exploration Fund and received on a yearly basis yet other Egyptica for the Museum.

By the turn of the century still other Old World collections had been acquired: the H. W. Seton-Karr collection of flint and quartzite tools; a collection of 273 Egyptian objects assembled in Cairo by Emil Brugsch, curator of the Bulak Museum;[16] the Kyticas collection of 35 Egyptian bronzes;[17] and, a collection of prehistoric stone tools from Denmark. In 1904, the Ikeda collection of "rare, ancient, and modern art of Japan and China" was added.[18] Moreover, collections formed by other members of the family had been given to the Museum: Mrs. Stanford's sister Anna Maria Lathrop Hewes bequeathed a large collection of Egyptian objects and contemporary art works formed by her husband, David Hewes, in Cairo and Rome during the 1870s;[19] and by 1905, one of Governor Stanford's brothers, Thomas Welton Stanford, who lived in Melbourne, had presented more than 150 paintings, including a unique group by contemporary Australian artists.[20]

To these Museum acquisitions were being added, bit by bit, objects from the huge private art collection the Stanfords had been assembling since 1870 for residences they either owned or leased in Sacramento, San Francisco, Palo Alto, New York, and Washington. This collection included not simply family memorabilia and copies of the Old Masters, as has erroneously been repeated, but hundreds of American and European paintings, largely by contemporary artists, as well as a huge cache of photographs and glass negatives by A. A.

Hart, Eadweard Muybridge, A. P. Hill, and other photographers of the American West. Much still remained in the Stanfords' Nob Hill house awaiting eventual transfer to the Museum—in particular a group of sixteenth- and seventeenth-century Italian paintings acquired abroad—when Mrs. Stanford died unexpectedly in 1905.

After her death a series of disasters plagued the Museum, causing large numbers of objects to be lost. Catastrophe devastated the building in 1906, when the earthquake of April 18 leveled two wings, bringing down the Egyptian, Roman, and Asian galleries and shattering more than a thousand Cypriot pots. Three-quarters of the huge structure, much of which stood empty awaiting future acquisitions, was irreparably damaged. (See pp. 19–21.) But every department suffered in the aftermath of the quake, so much so, indeed, that there was never again a chance to evaluate the Collection's overall quality.

Destruction in the San Francisco home was far worse. Since Mrs. Stanford's estate had not yet been fully settled after her death the year before, roughly 125 paintings and perhaps two dozen sculptures had not yet been moved to Palo Alto. Among the materials destroyed were papers relating to the provenance and classification of her acquisitions, in particular, of the Italian paintings bought in Florence. All twenty-two of these Old Master paintings perished when the house burned to the ground the day after the tremor. (Suspicions of theft are raised by the presence in the Museum today of two nineteenth-century paintings inscribed with the notation that each had been rescued from the house in April 1906.) No trace of the Stanfords' oils by Elisabetta Sirani, Carlo Dolci, Guido Reni, or other Italian Baroque painters has ever been found, leaving in limbo the question of authenticity surrounding the group, which was purchased at a time when misattribution was a commonplace for master paintings acquired abroad.

Many American paintings, too, intended for the Museum by the terms of Mrs. Stanford's will, were destroyed with the San Francisco house, among them, William Keith's *Mount Diablo*, landscapes by Julian Rix and Raymond Dabb Yelland, genre paintings by William Hahn, Seymour Joseph Guy, and Enoch Wood Perry, and more than a dozen works by Thomas Hill. Contemporary European paintings had no better fate; gone with the elaborate furnishings on Nob Hill were two Bouguereaus and a Gérôme, not to mention paintings by Hugues Merle, Meyer von Bremen, Toulmouche, Worms, and many sentimentalizing Victorians.

Paintings already in Palo Alto fared better, since they were hung in the Museum's original, steel-reinforced central pavilion of 1891, which, as Paul Turner explains in his essay on the architecture of the Museum, still stands today and houses the present University Museum. (The portions that collapsed were slightly later constructions built of brick and mortar.) For the most part, works on canvas came through the disaster unscathed, only to endure fifty subsequent years of neglect in the ravaged building or, worse, the vagaries of changing taste.

With the death of Jane Stanford, the Museum's budget was sharply curtailed because it had not been given a separate endowment. And the University, busy with reconstruction of its main buildings after the quake, had little concern for a museum so vastly out of scale with its practical needs. In 1914, with funds given by Thomas Welton Stanford, plans were made to construct a new building at some distance from the old to serve as an art gallery for changing exhibitions. The faculty and its administrators showed little desire to salvage from the Museum's wreckage whatever could have served as the start of a new, academically useful collection. The remains of the building were allowed to fall into further disrepair, and all pretense of curatorship gradually ceased. The Museum was to be closed to the public and used as a laboratory for Stanford students. Shortly thereafter, the departments of anatomy, physiology, and bacteriology were moved into the building. Then, during the 1924–25 academic year, various disciplines in the biological sciences department—botany, entomology, and zoology—were moved to the Museum's south wing. For more than fifty years this space housed extensive systematic collections of fish—in particular, the David Starr Jordan fish collection, one of the most important in the world—amphibians, reptiles, birds, mammals, invertebrates, and insects. The collection of plants, the Dudley Herbarium, which was also housed there, has since become the ninth largest in the United States and Canada and now resides at the California Academy of Sciences. (In 1939, praise for Palo Alto's collection of invertebrates and fishes elicited the only mention of the Stanford Museum in Laurence Vail Coleman's critical study, *The Museum in America*.) The plans at one time in the late 1920s and early 1930s were to include the geology and anthropology collections with the other biological holdings, in order to convert the entire building to a museum of natural history.[21] Stanford University's emphasis on the sciences at the expense of the humanities is aptly illustrated by the use that was made of the structure from the time of Mrs. Stanford's death until its rejuvenation as an art museum under the directorship of Lorenz Eitner in the 1960s.

BEFORE AND AFTER THE SAN
FRANCISCO EARTHQUAKE

Photographs on preceding page:

9 (above) *The Museum's lobby in 1905.*

10 (below, left) *The lobby shortly after the San Francisco earthquake of April 18, 1906.*

11 (below, right) *Sculptures inside the building were smashed and, outside, one of the four statues on the parapet above the entrance fell to the ground.*

12 (above) *The south wing, built of brick and stone masonry in 1898, collapsed in the quake.*

13 (left) *The worst damage came in the Egyptian gallery which was located in the south wing.*

14 *On the Stanford quadrangle, a passerby observed that "Agassiz was great in the abstract but not in the concrete."*

15 Cypriot pots from the Cesnola collection were hard hit.

16 Throughout the building fragile objects were broken.

During Mrs. Stanford's lifetime, natural-history exhibits occupied a very small percentage of the total space, but it is difficult to say precisely how many objects the Museum contained in all. No inventory of the Collection had been made before the earthquake of 1906. The first attempt consisted of a card catalogue accompanied by a two-volume ledger of single-line entries, prepared in 1917 by Harry C. Peterson, the Museum's curator since 1900. An unmatriculated engineering student at Stanford when the job fell open, Peterson had worked directly for Mrs. Stanford during the first five years of his tenure, helping her in the installation of more than twenty galleries; after the earthquake he had worked long hours for months trying to set things right. Until 1917, when he was replaced by Pedro J. Lemos, he had had full responsibility for the building—installations, collections, and upkeep. His letters disclose a man of modest pretensions, fully aware of his shortcomings as a scholar, but persistent enough to ask questions of those more knowledgeable than he.

During 1916–17, Peterson catalogued 28,200 objects, concluding the list with forty Tanagra figurines from the Leland Stanford Junior Collection and painting red accession numbers on everything from Seton-Karr's gift of stone implements to Jane Stanford's Worth gowns. The inventory he prepared was as accurate as it could have been, given the twin circumstances of breakage and his own lack of knowledge about the cataloguing of certain types of objects.

Among those who assisted him in classifying what remained of the Egyptian, Chinese, and Japanese holdings were three experts called in by Ray Lyman Wilbur, president of the University from 1916 to 1941. (When responsibility for the Museum was transferred from the University's board of trustees to the academic departments, an exhaustive effort to record the Museum's contents was undertaken at Wilbur's request.) These three experts were A. H. Sayce, an Oxford Near Eastern specialist, Carl Whiting Bishop, an authority on Chinese art, who was then curator of the Philadelphia Museum's Far Eastern department and later associate curator of the Freer Gallery, and Hogitara Ineda, a specialist in Japanese art. Their report found the collections "exceptionally pleasing . . . and far above the average in quality with a great many rare and unique articles."[22]

Yet discouragingly many of these works were among the thousands of objects from the original collection that were lost, sold, or given away, primarily during the period 1918–52, when the building's storage areas, unlit and without security, became a quarry for local collectors and dealers. While the university museums at Harvard, Yale, Princeton, Pennsylvania, and Oberlin developed into active centers of scholarship and attracted art collections of world importance during these decades, the Stanford Museum simply faded from existence.

In 1945, with the resignation of Peterson's successor, Pedro Lemos, the Museum was closed so that an inventory might again be undertaken. At this time it was determined by the art department that paintings and sculptures lacking in aesthetic merit might be sold. This was done during the academic year 1951–52, when valiant efforts were made to resurrect part of the building as an art museum and money was in short supply. An enormous accumulation of worthless material was disposed of, but so too were paintings and sculptures from the original family collection judged now to be of higher aesthetic value than it was believed in the 1950s. Among the American paintings were works by Albert Bierstadt, William Bradford, Norton Bush, Thomas Hill, and Richard LaBarre Goodwin. In the main, buyers' names were unrecorded.

The present reconstruction of the Museum's original holdings is based largely on documents and publications that have been ferreted out of basement closets and old filing cabinets in the Museum. Additional information has been found in newspaper accounts, old Museum catalogues, annual reports, family letters, and other archival sources at Stanford. Although occasional discrepancies occur between these pre-1906 records and Peterson's inventory of 1917, on the whole, his card catalogue is accurate as far as it goes. Of course, Peterson very much wished to broaden his knowledge, as inexperienced curators in many museums were setting out to do at this time, and he faulted the University for reneging on promises of two sabbatical leaves that would have taken him to museums on the East Coast for study. Moreover, it saddened Peterson to hear visitors complain about the Museum's poor condition, for it was a criticism he shared, blaming the neglect on a lack of funds. Commenting on the change in a letter to a friend, Peterson wrote that things were very different without Mrs. Stanford: "It's like a diet of sawdust after a feast of peaches and cream."[23]

The Stanford Family Collection

'. . . if not the best, the best that money can buy'

A note about the Stanfords' houses:

THROUGHOUT *their marriage, Leland and Jane Stanford collected art for the many houses in which they spent their lives together. Their favorite residence was the one in Sacramento where Leland Stanford Junior was born and to which his parents hoped to return after the former governor had retired from the presidency of the Central Pacific Railroad. After the Railroad's offices were moved from Sacramento to San Francisco, the Stanfords made their home on Nob Hill in the city. While living there, they acquired a country place in Palo Alto, thirty-five miles to the south, where Stanford could pursue his avocation of breeding horses. Although the Stanfords started their collection with paintings by artists working close to home, a trip east to the Philadelphia Centennial accelerated the collecting of European art, continued during trips to England and the Continent. The Stanfords also acquired art objects for the New York mansion they leased on Fifth Avenue and for the house they bought in Washington when Stanford served as senator. After the death of their son, Leland and Jane Stanford wanted to do something in his honor. For the Leland Stanford Junior Museum, they amassed a larger collection than ever with the intention of filling "the grandest museum in the world."*

17 The Sacramento house, about 1862, with Leland and Jane Stanford on the stoop, Jane's sister Anna Maria Lathrop at the window. Photograph by Alfred A. Hart.

SACRAMENTO

Picture buying, as William Dean Howells observed in his novel *The Rise of Silas Lapham* (1885), is a stage in a rich man's development that follows close upon the decoration of his house. And so it was with Leland Stanford, who began to buy American paintings in a serious way in 1871, the year of the completion of extensive remodeling on the Sacramento house the ex-governor and his wife had owned for ten years. Originally built as a two-story Georgian (17) by Seth Babson, the architect of the Crocker Art Gallery, the house was renovated for the Stanfords by Nathaniel Goodell, a leading architect of the time.[1] Goodell added a basement, a ballroom, and a mansard roof in the Second Empire style. The next year, when all was in place, its owners called in Eadweard Muybridge to photograph the decor, inside and out (18–20). In the Muybridge prints are seen the beginnings of Stanford's fine collection of paintings by artists working in San Francisco during the decade immediately following the Civil War.

Two landscapes by the celebrated American painter Albert Bierstadt were among the first paintings the Stanfords acquired for the house. *Yosemite Valley* was based on sketches Bierstadt had made during his first visit to California in 1863. His presence at that time was crucial to the development of the California school as Dwight Miller has remarked in his essay on the school. Bierstadt "was the first impressive talent among American painters to dedicate himself to California scenery—his work gave the strongest impetus to the whole development."[2] Drawn to the Far West by the wonders of Yosemite, Bierstadt immediately set out for the Valley, taking with him two San Francisco painters he had known in Europe, Enoch Wood Perry and Virgil Williams. Making oil sketches on the scene and finishing them later in his studio, Bierstadt recapitulated Yosemite's magnificence in a series of impressive views (22). The version Stanford bought was probably completed in Rome in 1868. Its general composition, described in the *San Francisco Bulletin,*[3] was not unfamiliar:

In the distance are represented the Cathedral Rocks, which the setting sun throws into bold relief, and between which a small strip of sunlight is thrown, striking the few trees in the foreground. The

PHOTOGRAPHS BY EADWEARD
MUYBRIDGE OF THE
SACRAMENTO HOUSE IN 1872

18 Front view with new mansard roof.

19 Jane Stanford and her sister Anna Maria Lathrop (right) *at the billiard table with Leland, aged four.*

24

combination of light and shade is so artistic that one imagines he can almost see the shadows play up and down the mountain sides and along the ground. The weird tone of the background is strikingly heightened by the masterly handling of the strip of sunshine.

Stanford also owned works by Bierstadt's traveling companions, Perry, a genre painter who had studied in Düsseldorf like Bierstadt himself and many other American artists of the mid-century, and Williams, a figure painter and the first president of the San Francisco Art Institute. But Perry's *Hospitality* and *Words of Comfort* and Williams's *Italian Fisherman and His Daughter* were destroyed on Nob Hill in 1906 together with Bierstadt's *Yosemite Valley.*

Stanford's second Bierstadt, *Happy Hunting Ground,* which was transferred to the Museum before 1906 and sold in 1951 to an unidentified buyer, was also described:

drawn from imagination, [it] represents the Indian's ideal of his Happy Hunting Ground.... It seems to be an interior abode, communicating with the outside world by a small mouth, like that of a cave, through which water flows. Indians are seen peacefully gliding inward in a cave. The setting sun streams in and floods the foliage and trees, bringing them out in bold and masterly prominence. Those in the foreground are worked with great fidelity.[4]

The Stanfords bought the two paintings from an artist who had achieved both great critical acclaim and also great financial success—an artist who was a power in the art world. In September 1871, the newly formed San Francisco Art Association made the most of Bierstadt's return to the city by staging a special reception at the Snow and Roos Gallery to mark the *vernissage* of his new work.[5] Stanford bought Bierstadt's two paintings on the spot. It is likely that Bierstadt influenced Stanford's later choices, given the superlative quality of the family's holdings in American art. Of course, it was entirely typical of Stanford's dealings throughout his life, not simply with painters but also with all those involved in the arts, to go directly to the best available professionals and to respond sensibly to their advice.

At the Snow and Roos reception, Bierstadt made a point of expressing his delight with the works of the San Francisco Art Association members that were displayed together with his own. By then, the city's artists were thriving, and railroad men like Stanford, Mark Hopkins, Collis P. Huntington, and Charles Crocker (the Big Four) were among their supporters, along with Edwin B. Crocker, the brother of Charles, who was their legal counsel for the railroad.

Among the painters admired by this group was Norton Bush, whose works were also purchased by Stanford for the Sacramento house. The little oval view of a *Mountain Landscape,* 1869 (21), still in the Museum today, appears in Muybridge's photograph of the parlor (20) as does *Nicaragua,* which was sold by the University

20 The parlor with two oval paintings by Norton Bush, Mountain Landscape (left) *and* Nicaragua.

21 Norton Bush, Mountain Landscape, *1869, oil on canvas.* (sm 12162)

22 Albert Bierstadt, Yosemite
Valley, *1868, is similar in
composition and date to the
Stanfords' Bierstadt destroyed in
1906.* (Oakland Museum)

in 1951. Like Stanford, Bush had crossed Central America by way of Nicaragua, coming to California a year later, in 1853, sketching as he traveled. In San Francisco, during the 1860s and 1870s, Bush executed the series of tropical scenes that made him the most successful painter in the West of a genre popularized in the East by Frederick Church and others. Born in Rochester, New York, and a former student of Jasper Cropsey, Bush was one of dozens of artists from upstate New York patronized by the Stanfords, whose origins were there. Another painting by Bush, *Valley Landscape,* 1867, is currently on view at Stanford. A fourth was put up for sale in the fund-raising campaign of the 1950s, and its location is now unknown.

Bierstadt and Stanford became special friends, and in January 1873, the artist and his family were invited to Sacramento for a visit. Perhaps it was on this occasion that Bierstadt signed and dedicated to Stanford his lithograph of the Rocky Mountains (1864), which hung for many years in the Sacramento house.[6] Surely it was in 1873 that the artist's sister-in-law, Esther Mayer, confided a few catty remarks to her journal, describing Mrs. Stanford as a very large woman who wore magnificent jewels—"such emeralds and diamonds!" The group was together again in August 1879, this time forming a luncheon party of twenty in New York aboard the *Britannic* on the occasion of the Bierstadt's return from Europe. Again Bierstadt's sister was impressed by Mrs. Stanford's jewels: "She wore the biggest emerald solitaire earrings I ever saw!"[7] (See illustration p. 68.)

SAN FRANCISCO: The American Collection

B Y THE LATE 1870s, some of the Stanford fortune had been put into the building of a second house: in 1874, a year after the offices of the Central Pacific Railroad were moved to San Francisco from Sacramento, Stanford became the first of the Big Four to build on Nob Hill. The architectural firm of Samuel C. Bugbee and Son designed the Italianate villa that once stood on the block bounded by California, Powell, Pine, and Mason. Constructed of cut stone on the ground floor, the upper walls of the mansion were apparently built of redwood covered with plaster. Again, when all was in place, Muybridge was called in to photograph the results (23). His pictures are all that remain of the house, for it was completely destroyed by the fire that swept the city in the aftermath of the earthquake of 1906.

Its storied wonders once held not only an art gallery in which to display the growing collection, but also an interior decor that harked back, in its elaborate iconographic program, to the merchant palaces of the Renaissance—indeed, as the *San Francisco Chronicle* put it, "but few palaces of Europe excell it" (24–28). Executed in 1876, the decoration was the work of G. G. Gariboldi, an Italian-born fresco painter who was given carte blanche by Mrs. Stanford for its design and the assistance of sixteen craftsmen for its execution. But let the *Chronicle* continue:

We begin at the entrance of the mansion, which is up a noble flight of stone stairs, flanked on each side at the first rise by tall, square pillars, surmounted by gas lamps of elegant patterns. From the stairs we enter the vestibule, which is executed in mosaic, with a centre figure representing "Fidelity," typified by a stalwart hound seated quietly at vigilant rest, and as if guarding the entrance to the house. The entrance hall is decorated with frescoes, worked in light and shade, in the Greco-Italian style. The ceilings are in white and gold blended with blue, of which the centre piece contains a large picture representing "Abundance" and the scripture "Welcome to Visitors" with the Latin legend *Pax Vobis* (Peace be with you).[8]

The vestibule opened into "a noble rotunda," which ascended to the second story (24). The woodwork on the windows and doors of both floors was by the firm of Pottier and Stymus. The rotunda's mosaic floor was inset with the twelve signs of the zodiac, its ceiling, high above, with figures in the "Etruscan" style, "representing incidents of Etruscan home life." Encircling the mezzo rotunda were frescoes, in the "Greco-Italian" style, of the seven days of the week. Above, in the rotunda's upper hall, the cove of the ceiling was embellished in the "Neo-Pompeian" style and divided into eight large panels depicting the four corners of the globe—Africa, Asia, Europe, and America. In between, four emblematic figures represented fine arts, mechanics, agriculture, and

23 The San Francisco house photographed by Eadweard Muybridge in 1878.

PHOTOGRAPHS BY EADWEARD
MUYBRIDGE OF THE SAN
FRANCISCO HOUSE IN 1878

*24 The upper rotunda with
lunette frescoes of* America *and*
The Fine Arts *by Gariboldi.*

*25 Sitting room with Cogswell's
portrait of Leland Stanford Junior
and Nahl's* Mexican Lady with
Bird.

*26 View from the dining room,
with Nahl's* Peacock, *through the
art gallery to the Pompeian room.*

*27 The Pompeian room in the
Adamesque revival style with
furnishings acquired at the
Philadelphia Centennial.
Benzoni's* Diana *and* Apollo *in
the adjacent art gallery.*

literature. Just below them on the walls of the second floor—front stage, as it were, in the drama of time and space—hung the dour portraits of the Stanford's ancestors, plain fare in the elaborate cosmology at California and Powell.

Other paintings, together with sculptures and objects, were placed not only in the art gallery (32), which opened off the rotunda, but throughout the house. Charles Christian Nahl's *Peacock* hung in the dining room beneath a frescoed ceiling (26). Nahl, born to a distinguished family of artists in Cassel, Germany, had come to California in the Gold Rush and was a great favorite

*28 The library with portraits of
Leland and Jane Stanford by
William Cogswell destroyed with
the house in 1906.*

29 Charles Christian Nahl,
Mexican Lady with a Bird,
c. 1872, oil on canvas. (SM 12046)

30 Charles Christian Nahl,
Hummingbirds, *1876, oil on
canvas.* (SM 69.259)

31 William Cogswell, Leland
Stanford Junior, *1872, oil on
canvas.* (SM 14892)

*32 (below) The art gallery with
Thomas Hill's* Mount Shasta *and
William Keith's* Upper Kern
River *on the left-hand wall; a
replica of Raphael's* Madonna of
the Chair *in the far right corner.*

of the Stanfords. Both *Mexican Lady with a Bird* (29), which hung in the sitting room of the Nob Hill house in 1878 (25), and *Hummingbirds,* 1876 (30), display the bravura technique that must have made Nahl's flashy illusionism seem sheer magic to collectors in the West. He was probably the only artist in America capable at that time of achieving certain *trompe l'oeil* effects. Years later, Jane Stanford bought for the Museum from J. O. Coleman two paintings by Nahl in an entirely different style, the famous *Saturday Night at the Mines,* 1856, and *Crossing the Plains,* 1851.[9] Both are still at Stanford, but Nahl's *Peacock* was destroyed in the fire. (See p. 69.)

33 Thomas Hill, Yosemite
Valley, *1876, was owned by*
Leland Stanford when it was
exhibited at the Philadelphia
Centennial. (Oakland Museum)

Another important San Francisco artist whose works Stanford bought in the 1870s was William Keith, a friend of the naturalist John Muir. Keith's *Mount Diablo* (destroyed,1906) hung in the main hall, his *Upper Kern River,* 1876 (34), in the art gallery. Like Bierstadt, Keith had studied in Düsseldorf, and at this point in his career he was still painting in its grandiloquent style. Now at the Stanford Museum, *Upper Kern River* is a dramatic depiction of the majestic sweep of the Sierra, opening up to the eye of the beholder the magnificence of the western setting, its lofty vistas. An even more inspirational attitude was expressed in the masterly *View of Yosemite Valley (from Sentinal Dome),* 1876 (33), by Stanford's favorite artist, the English-born painter Thomas Hill.

Stanford's admiration for the paintings of Thomas Hill resulted in nearly twenty-five landscapes of California scenery for the Nob Hill house; and, although the views varied from Emerald Bay, Tallac, and Fallen Leaf Lake to Mount Shasta and the Coast Range, scenes of the Sierra predominated. In 1875, Stanford spoke sugges-

tively to Hill about his feeling for the mountain range:

[He talked] at considerable length, of his troubles and trials while building the railroad across the Sierras, the great amount of time he spent in that wild region while burrowing through the mountains around Donner Lake, which he graphically described. How often he wandered to a very high point which overlooked the great work and the Lake in the beautiful valley 3,000 feet below.[10]

If somewhat elliptic in discussing his experience, Stanford was so affected by his recollection that he commissioned Hill to paint Donner Lake from that very point. The scene was a favorite with railroad men for its association with not only the completion of the railroad to the summit but also the tragedy of the Donner Party trapped by snow in the winter of 1846. Collis P. Huntington had commissioned such a painting from Bierstadt, *Donner Lake from the Summit* (35), in 1871, and no doubt Stanford had it in mind when he ordered a nearly identical painting from Hill a few years later. Eventually destroyed in the earthquake, Hill's *Donner Lake* was

34 *William Keith,* Upper
Kern River, *1876, visible in
Muybridge's photograph of the
art gallery, is one of a group of*
*paintings by Keith of the
headwaters of California's
rivers.* (SM 12057)

35 *Albert Bierstadt,* Donner
Lake, *commissioned by Collis
Huntington in 1870, was the
model for Thomas Hill's painting*
*of 1876, owned by Stanford and
later destroyed in the earthquake.*
(New-York Historical Society)

fully described in the *Alta California:*

The time is about 9 a.m.; the formation of the country and the color of the rocks being such that in the general opinion of artists, no tolerable picture could be painted of the scene with any fidelity to nature, at a later hour of the day.... On the right, is the steep mountain side with the line of the railroad cut into the rocky cliffs.[11]

The same article goes on to point out that both paintings of Donner Lake from the summit "were taken from near the same point, and at nearly the same hour of the day" and that the comparison was not unfavorable to Hill. Furthermore, he had done the work for only $6,000 while Bierstadt, it was rumored, had charged Huntington $20,000 for his view of the rugged scene.

In their patronage of Hill, Bierstadt, and other artists who portrayed mountain ranges of the West, Stanford and Huntington exemplified the commercial class—men who made their money in transport—that generally provided the greatest support to American landscape painters.[12] Despite all the attention railroad men paid to contemporary European art—and Stanford, like Huntington, paid his share—they remained the best patrons of American art, of all sorts, throughout the latter decades of the nineteenth century. Financiers and merchants like August Belmont and A. T. Stewart may have paid the highest prices for all works of art, but railroad men were the most loyal patrons of American landscapists. After all, who knew better the exhilaration of the land than those who had surveyed it for the railway? And who could better appreciate the sublime reaches of the West than those who had tamed them for the Central Pacific?

Who, indeed, cared more about bringing travelers west on the transcontinental railroad than those who owned it? Heroic in scope, size, and execution, the sweeping views of the West that the Big Four bought from Keith, Bierstadt, Hill, and others were the best advertisements for the wonders to be seen on the Pacific Coast. As a major patron, Stanford, like Huntington and the rest, seems to have had the privilege, at a rather late date in the history of art, of dictating not only the contents of the paintings he commissioned, but also their size. Like Keith's *Upper Kern River* and Bierstadt's *Donner Lake,* Hill's painting was to be ten feet in length by six in height. When it was completed, Hill reported, Stanford was entirely satisfied with the results.

There was one interesting complication, however. On one of the many visits Stanford and his wife and son paid to Hill's studio, Stanford saw that Hill was working on the great view of Yosemite Valley, which the artist planned to send to the Philadelphia Centennial. Stanford, who planned to visit the fair with his family, objected that the Donner Lake painting should go instead. But Hill discouraged him, saying that its subject was not one to bring him the honors he was seeking. "Why not?" Stanford asked. Hill replied that a picture of a railroad was "unpoetic" and might hurt his prospects.[13] Thereupon, Stanford bought *Yosemite Valley,* too, and sent both paintings to the Centennial. *Yosemite* was awarded a medal for landscape painting, and Stanford was given the satisfaction of seeing his two canvases serve in Philadelphia as the biggest billboards of the sublime Valley.

Stanford's shrewd eye for the mythic effect of visual imagery is implied by two huge figural paintings he soon commissioned from Hill: a portrait of three generations of Stanfords together with their young friends on the lawn of the Palo Alto house in the spring of 1878 (37) and the celebratory *Driving of the Last Spike at Promontory, Utah, on May 10, 1869* (38), executed from about 1875 to 1880. For historical subjects of such specific definition, it comes as a surprise to learn that each is an artistic contrivance. At Palo Alto by 1878, for example, Stanford's mother, who appears in the painting at the Governor's right, had been dead for several years, his brother Thomas Welton Stanford had never seen the town, and Charles Lathrop, his brother-in-law, had remained in New York throughout the year. The portrait of young Leland, whose tenth birthday on May 14 the painting probably celebrates (and perhaps there was such a croquet party on the lawn that day) was lifted directly from a photograph (36) as were many of the other figures. Although the boy is surrounded in the domestic scene by pretty little children and young folk of assorted ages, the truth is that he was an only child; and none of his cousins matched in age the plump babies intermingled with

36 The photograph of Leland Stanford Junior at the age of ten was one of many photographs of family members used by Thomas Hill for Palo Alto Spring, *1878.*

adults of the Stanford and Lathrop families. What is in earnest, it would seem, is the myth of domestic bliss and fecundity that the artist creates. Thomas Hill stands to the right of the *pater familias,* Stanford the generous provider.

In the case of the *Last Spike,* however, Hill has left an explicit account of Stanford's self-promotion. For after working for five years on the eight-by-twelve foot canvas, the artist was dismayed to find that his patron refused to pay for it. So Hill published a little booklet, *History of the*

'Spike Picture' and why it is still in my possession, in which he set forth what he described as the facts of the case. The project had begun innocently enough with Stanford's summons to the artist, saying that "he had a great desire to see a grand historical painting of the driving of the last spike, and wanting to know if Hill thought that he could paint such a picture "with portraits of all the prominent characters present on that occasion." But after Hill began working on the painting, Stanford changed his point of view, asking Hill to paint *out* all of his enemies and to paint *in* all of his friends, never mind whether they had been present on the spectacular occasion or not. When discussion turned to the easterner Thomas C. Durant, vice-president of the Union Pacific, who drove the silver spike into the special laurel railroad tie at Promontory, Stanford demanded that this attribute be removed: "Nobody has a hammer but me."

Hill referred in passing to drawings, sketched earlier by a sculptor, "in which Mr. Stanford was represented coming out of the clouds on a locomotive, and in many other god-like attitudes figurative of the life and doings of the Governor." If Hill was bemused by Stanford's egotism, Charles Crocker was outraged. Seeing the revised version of the *Last Spike* for the first time, Crocker took immediate offense. "What the d——d nonsense is that?" Hill quoted him as saying. Hill explained the situation to him and told Crocker how important it was for him to sit for a portrait that would be included "in the great work." Instead, Crocker walked out "with malice in his eye." From that moment, Stanford gave Hill a wide berth, sending word that he did not wish to buy any more pictures from him. Hill's friends urged the artist to force the Governor to justice, but remembering Stanford's previous generosity, "which was liberal in the extreme," Hill did not prosecute, though he did pursue Stanford for many years in an attempt to get him to buy the work.[14] Hill ended his pamphlet by writing that he had learned to his sorrow the truth of the adage "Put not your faith in princes."

37 (fold-out) Thomas Hill, Palo Alto Spring, *1878, oil on canvas. From the left: Jane Stanford seated next to her mother, her husband's mother, her husband and son. Standing behind them are Anna Maria Lathrop, an unidentified man, and the artist Thomas Hill. Beyond them are seated Leland Stanford's brothers Josiah*

and Thomas Welton and an unidentified man with Jane's brother Henry Lathrop standing behind them.

Of the croquet players, only the kneeling Josiah Winslow Stanford is known. The three girls may be Jane's nieces, Jennie, Christina, and Aimée, the daughters of Daniel Lathrop. (SM 14945)

32

38 Thomas Hill, Driving of the Last Spike, *1875–80, oil on canvas.* (California Railroad Museum)

40 The historic locomotive, "The Governor Stanford," entered the Museum in 1918. It is now on view in the California Railroad Museum, Sacramento.

39 The Last Spike. (sm)

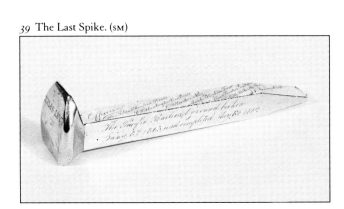

Throughout the years that Hill worked on Stanford's commissions, the Governor also engaged artists who specialized in the sporting life to portray champion trotters at the Palo Alto Stock Farm. In the days when trotters, not thoroughbreds, were the kings and queens of the American turf, Stanford owned one of the finest stables in the world for their breeding and training. Purchased in 1876 for the scientific rearing of the trotting horse, the Farm later became the setting for the University. In 1891, when students were entering for the first time, every world's record for the trotting horse—from yearling to five-year-old—was held by a horse bred at Palo Alto and trained under Stanford's guidance. His system of training the colt by fast workouts at a young age produced remarkable results for some twenty years—from 1876 to 1896, the heyday of the Stock Farm (41).

Artists commemorated the feats and beauty of Stanford's horses in paintings and prints and, uniquely, in photographs of their attitudes in motion. Today, the Museum holds a sizable collection of the sporting scenes that formerly hung on the walls of the Palo Alto house. When Jane Stanford was alive, the Museum was the repository for hundreds of photographs as well; but because the majority of these were subsequently transferred to the University Archives, today the Museum retains only the works of Eadweard Muybridge.[15]

Muybridge's cinematographic experiments on the Palo Alto track made a horse named Occident the first

42 Occident *by John Cameron in a lithograph published by* *Currier and Ives in 1873.* (Private collection)

American movie star. The little brown gelding lived a rags-to-riches story: he was a dirt horse in Sacramento, carting construction debris, when Stanford discovered him in 1870, worked with him, trained him, and in 1873 saw him break the record for the mile—the first horse from California to become a world champion. Muybridge photographed him standing still with his driver Yank Smith in 1872 and in 1877 as the Horse in Motion.[16]

Occident—the California Wonder—was the subject also of prints published by Currier and Ives in 1873 and 1876 by John Cameron (42), one of the country's best horse portraitists, and Thomas Worth, an illustrator in New York City who specialized in racing scenes. Overall,

41 *The Palo Alto Stock Farm in the 1880s. Detail of a photograph by Archibald Treat.*

some five hundred surviving prints by Currier and Ives catch the fever pitch of track and road at a time when 13 million horses were at work in the United States. Stanford's goal was to produce for this market a horse that would make the family wheels fly, its sleds glide as Silas Lapham's did in the novel by Howells:

Nothing in the immutable iron of Lapham's face betrayed his sense of triumph as the mare left everything behind her on the road.... [E]xcept for the rush of her feet, the mare was as silent as the people behind her; the muscles of her back and thighs worked more and more swiftly, like some mechanism responding to an alien force, and she shot to the end of the course, grazing a hundred encountered and rival sledges in her passage, but unmolested by the policemen who ... were not the sort of men to interfere with trotting like that.[17]

Stanford's eye for the conformation that yielded speed was demonstrated when he bought the Hambletonian stallion Electioneer in Orange County, New York, not far from where Stanford had grown up. Purchased for stud, Electioneer was the most natural trotter his trainer Charles Marvin had ever seen, with "perfect rolling action both in front and behind."[18] By a larger percentage than any other stud that had ever lived, this stallion sired offspring naturally gifted with the ability to trot fast. According to Marvin, "they trot low, have no waste action, and gather speed quickly and smoothly."

Sunol, the most famous, still holds the record for the high-wheeled sulky: in 1891, racing as a five-year-old, she made the world's fastest time for all ages, 2:08 1/4. That year her picture was painted by a little-known artist named Jerome Casey (43). Another champion was Palo Alto, the Governor's favorite horse, photographed, also in 1891, by Andrew P. Hill. Both the mare and the stallion were sired by Electioneer in union with thoroughbred dams, controversial breeding that Stanford believed was the best way to infuse the standard-bred trotter with speed. When the bay gelding Fred Crocker, son of Electioneer, raced at the California State Fair in a stake race for two-year-olds, it was the first time anyone had seen a horse that young trot the mile under 2:30. The next year, in 1881, Fred Crocker was portrayed by Kirby Van Zandt (44), the Albany artist from whom the Stanfords commissioned at least nine paintings. Apparently, Jane Stanford had made the first contact with Van Zandt in 1875, when she had him copy in oil a pastel of her father Dyer Lathrop, a prosperous Albany merchant who died in 1855. Over the next six years or so, Van

43 Jerome Casey, Sunol, *1891, oil on canvas.* (SM 63.93)

44 Thomas Kirby Van Zandt, Fred Crocker, *1881, oil on canvas.* (SM 62.297)

45 Thomas Kirby Van Zandt, Goldsmith Maid Driven by Budd Doble, *1876, oil on canvas.* (SM 63.108)

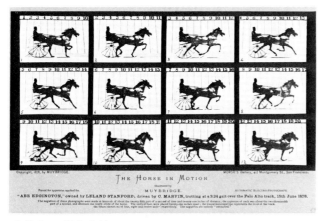

46 Eadweard Muybridge,
The Horse in Motion: Abe
Edgington, *1878.* (SM 13929)

Zandt provided paintings of Mrs. Stanford's birthplace, the boyhood home of Governor Stanford, Elm Grove Farm, 1880, and Leland Stanford Junior, with ice skates near an Albany pond, inscribed "February 1880." (See Chronology.)

Among Van Zandt's five horse paintings are two that put us in touch with an especially colorful bit of Americana. The first was a picture of a horse not owned by Stanford, Goldsmith Maid, portrayed with sulky and the famous driver Budd Doble in 1876 (45).

> Blue are the skies of opening day;
> The bordering turf is green with May;
> The sunshine's golden gleam is thrown
> On sorrell, chestnut, bay, and roan. . . .

In Oliver Wendell Holmes's poem of that year, "How

47 Thomas Kirby Van Zandt,
Abe Edgington, Driven by

Budd Doble, *1877, oil on canvas.*
(SM 63.106)

the Old Horse Won the Bet," Holmes pitted Budd Doble's nag in the trio that raced the parson's poor old bay, "the same that drew the one-horse shay." In real life, Goldsmith Maid driven by Doble had been the winner of several important trials; she was one of the great queens of the turf, following Lady Suffolk and Flora Temple in the pantheon of trotters. All three were featured in the assault on the two-minute mile.

Moreover, Budd Doble, "whose catarrhal name so fills the nasal trump of fame," as Holmes puts it in the poem, also raced horses for Stanford. The year that the poem was published, he took the gray gelding Abe Edgington (47) east for the campaign of 1876. Stoutly built, high in the withers, and lofty in carriage, Edgington attracted attention wherever he went. (He was another star of Muybridge's *Horse in Motion* series [46], but the record shows that he made a better film star than racer.) In September, Van Zandt made a sketch of him in crayon and wash in a pose which the artist finished as an oil painting more than a year later (47). The juxtaposition is of interest because it suggests that Van Zandt painted his horse pictures from nature, and not from photographs, regardless of the stereotyped posture of the driver and sulky. Indeed, it was said of Van Zandt that he "disdained all aids, or so-called helps to his art, and painted entirely from nature."[19] At the time of his death in 1886, when the writer of his obituary made these remarks, Van Zandt had been noted for forty years as an animal painter of extraordinary ability.

On a later visit to Paris, Stanford's astute and thorough knowledge of the horse—in particular, of the horse in motion—gave him entrée to the studio of the celebrated painter Ernest Meissonier, a specialist in both portraiture and battle and genre scenes with horses. When Stanford attempted to arrange for a portrait of himself, Meissonier was at first reluctant to accept the commission. But when Stanford began to tell him about his horses, Meissonier was intrigued. What captivated him in particular was the scientific proof that Stanford was able to put before his eyes: the Muybridge photographs of the horse in motion. The fast lenses of the twenty-four cameras used by Stanford and Muybridge in the famous experiments at the Palo Alto Stock Farm corrected errors about the position of the animal's legs that painters had made for centuries. Above all, it demonstrated that when a horse is entirely off the ground, the legs are bunched up under the trunk and not flung out from the center. In his portrait of Leland Stanford, 1881, Meissonier made the Muybridge album one of the Governor's attributes—an icon of nineteenth-century Scientific Realism (56).

SAN FRANCISCO: The European Collection

WITH RESPECT TO European paintings, the Stanfords' taste was similar to that of collectors on the East Coast. Works by the same contemporary European artists promoted by the New York art dealer Samuel P. Avery during the 1870s and bought by such clients as William H. Vanderbilt, John Taylor Johnston, and A. T. Stewart hung, by 1882, on the walls of the Stanfords' Nob Hill house—Bouguereau and Gérôme to be sure, but also a raft of prominent contemporaries who have slipped from sight over the years only to reappear recently as the flotsam of the auction trade: Chaigneau, Chierici, Col, Comte, de Haas, Markelbach, Hugues Merle, Meyer von Bremen, Piot, Portielje, Toulmouche, Worms, and the inevitable Eugen Verboeckhoven, the Belgian artist who specialized in barnyard scenes. A possession prized by the Stanfords was *On the Ice in Holland* by Frederik Kaemmerer, the Dutch artist popularized by Avery in the United States and sought by collectors as a surrogate for Gérôme, who had been Kaemmerer's teacher. Another Avery favorite whose work was owned by Stanford was the German artist Ludwig Knaus. Paintings by Knaus were selling for high prices in New York as early as 1864 when Avery auctioned *The Truant* for $1,675. (At this time, the going prices at auction for paintings by living European artists was about $300.)

In their choice of subject matter, the Stanfords shared the preference of the age for anecdotal and sentimental genre scenes. Titles tell the story and add to the rich vein of social history that the recent revival of interest in Victorian art has exposed: *Mother's Coming* by Mose Bianchi, *The Sick Mother* and *The Nurse* by Gaetano Chierici, *Charity* and *Family Love* by Hugues Merle, *Considering the Answer* by the Dutch genre painter Portielje, *You Mustn't Touch* (or, *The New Arrival*) by Meyer von Bremen, *All About Her Conquests* by Auguste Toulmouche, and so on. Typical also were subjects treating art and artists: Berker's *Picture Dealer,* for example, Markelbach's *The Critics,* and the *Courtship of Salvator Rosa* by the Milanese painter Pietro Bouvier. Oriental themes, too, had their place in Gérôme's canvas of a Turkish woman, *The Veil,* and in Pio Bianchi's watercolor *In the Seraglio.*

Literary and historical subjects were also favored by the Stanfords. Van Lerius's *Fair Rosamond in the Labyrinth* hung near a scene, based on Bulwer's play *Richelieu,* by the American painter J. Beaufrain Irving. *Feeding the Carp at Fontainebleau* by the painter Pierre Charles Comte, known for his Realist recreations of sixteenth-century court life, appeared not far from J. A. Kruseman's *Death of William the Silent,* purchased in Holland by Stanford on his first trip abroad. In 1888, after he had become senator, Stanford bought for the Washington house *The Departure of Princess Dagmar,* 1876, a painting set in the Court of Meissen during the thirteenth century by the Bohemian artist Vacslav Brozik. Brozik had exhibited the work at the Salon of 1877, and, as the Parisian dealer Sedelmeyer pointed out in the course of selling Stanford the painting for Fr 10,000 he had gone on to win gold medals at exhibitions in Antwerp, Berlin, Brussels, and Munich during the following decade. Brought to the Stanford Museum in the 1890s, Brozik's *Departure of Princess Dagmar* was subsequently sold to raise money for the renovation of the building.

Somewhat less typical, however, was the group of oils and watercolors of Italian scenes, executed largely by Italian artists and acquired by Jane Stanford on the Grand Tour of 1880–81: *View of Florence* and *View of Rome* by Agoshini; *Tending Sheep* by Daniele Bucciarelli; *Campagna at Rome* by Pietro Barucci; several watercolors by Finardi, including *The Conscript, Italian Peasant, Neapolitan Peasant, Roman Flower Girl, Roman Girl;* and a mosaic of the *Ruins of Pestum* by Claudio Rinaldi. One of the few paintings rescued from the San Francisco house before it was consumed by flames in 1906 was Franz Aerni's *Castel Sant'Angelo* commissioned by Mrs. Stanford in Rome in March of 1881 (48).

Religious motifs, another theme common to academically minded artists of the late-nineteenth century, had but one serious contender in the Stanfords' private art gallery, *A Christian Martyr Led to the Arena of the Coliseum* by Auguste Leloir. The painting was described by Earl Shinn in the account of Leland Stanford's Collection that appeared in Shinn's invaluable guide to the taste of the Gilded Age, *Art Treasures of America,* published in 1882. Leloir portrayed "a fair girl, whom a jailer pushes by the shoulder into the arena. . . . The wild beasts glare at her from their cages as she passes them; an ancient bearded martyr comes behind, and the contrast between her seraphic face and the venerable countenance of the older sufferer is emphatic. He seems to regret that he can give to heaven such a few remaining years, while the maiden can offer the whole rich treasure of her life."[20]

Of course the Stanfords were not the only collectors in San Francisco buying what was fashionable in Paris and New York. Shinn also cited the collections of Mrs. D. D. Colton and Mrs. George Hearst, as well as those of A. E.

*48 Franz Aerni's oil of the Castel
Sant'Angelo, commissioned by
Jane Stanford in Rome in 1881,
was painted from a picturesque
spot on the Tiber made famous by
Corot.* (SM 80.2)

Head, Irving Scott, and Charles Crocker, who owned a Boldini, a Cabanel, and Gérôme's *Sword-Dance in a Café*. Crocker's son William Henry, born in 1861, went on to buy a Delacroix, a Courbet, a Degas, a Pissarro, and two paintings by Monet, *Poplars* and *Haystack*. For by the end of the century, tastes had changed and many Americans were buying Impressionist paintings.

As for others of the Big Four, it is known that Huntington, who was collecting American paintings during the 1870s, became active in New York auctions just after his marriage to Arabella Worsham in 1884. His favorite painting, *The Missionary Story* by Jean Vibert, was purchased in 1886 for the high price of $25,500 from the Mary Jane Morgan sale. By 1896, however, the Huntingtons had added a Prud'hon, a Couture, and several works by Barbizon painters to their French holdings—Narcisse Diaz, Jules Dupré, and Theodore Rousseau—and the beginnings of the collection of eighteenth-century English portraits were seen in paintings by Gainsborough, Reynolds, Romney, and Raeburn.

Vermeer's *Guitar Player,* too, was acquired. When Huntington died in 1900 approximately two hundred of his paintings were willed to the Metropolitan Museum of Art in New York.

During the 1870s, however, by far the best collection of European paintings and drawings in northern California was the one assembled by the Stanfords' former Sacramento neighbors, Judge Edwin Bryant Crocker and his wife Margaret Rhodes Crocker, during their ten-month stay in Germany in 1870–71. They purchased about seven hundred paintings, including many by academically trained artists associated with Dresden, Munich, and Düsseldorf, together with other fine European paintings from the sixteenth to the eighteenth centuries. Even more impressive was the acquisition of more than a thousand Master drawings of superlative quality, all apparently acquired from the Dresden dealer Rudolph von Weigel. The E. B. Crockers' collection, together with their handsome art gallery, was given to the city of Sacramento in 1885.

EUROPE, 1880–81

IN THE LATE SPRING of 1880, Leland and Jane Stanford embarked on the first—and surely the happiest—of the five trips they took to Europe together.[21] Its purpose was primarily the education of young Leland, then a boy of twelve. After a summer together in England and France, Governor Stanford returned to the States for a winter of business, rejoining his family in Paris in June 1881. Meanwhile, traveling with a maid and a valet, Mrs. Stanford escorted her son on a grand tour, which took them to picture galleries and museums in Dresden, Berlin, Hamburg, Amsterdam, Antwerp, Brussels, and Paris before they headed south for Florence, Rome, Naples, and Pompeii. Following in the Crockers' footsteps, they spent three weeks in Dresden, a city whose collections date from 1560, when Elector Augustus I of Saxony founded his *Kunstkammer* or Cabinet of Curiosities on the top floor of the palace. By the late nineteenth century, its contents—everything from ostrich eggs to surgical instruments, including goblets, clocks, prints, paintings, and sculpture—had been dispersed into specialized museums for the education of the public. In the Picture Gallery, built in the 1850s next to the famous Zwinger, Mrs. Stanford was able to see Raphael's *Sistine Madonna,* a high point of the Victorian pilgrimage. She was subsequently to have it copied twice—with special permission from the king of Saxony—once for the Museum and once for the Roman Catholic cathedral in Sacramento. She already owned a copy of Raphael's *Madonna of the Chair,* visible in a photograph of the Nob Hill house in 1878, that may have been acquired from Woodward's Gardens in San Francisco (49).

The weather in Germany was bad, she wrote to her husband, and since her health had been a problem, she was anxious to get to Paris. On the train from Dresden to Berlin, it was so cold "you could see your breath."[22] (Not wanting to pay first-class fares for her servants, nor to be separated from them, she traveled in second.) She wrote that she was wearing her red woolen drawers and had bought a fur cape for the unheated cars. The weather improved, and the party made stops in Holland and Belgium. In the cathedral at Antwerp, Mrs. Stanford saw Rubens's great *Crucifixion,* confiding to her husband that until that moment she had never cared for pictures by the Flemish master.[23] She was learning. And as a side note in the history of taste, it is of interest to recall that Raphael and Rubens, with Titian, whose paintings Mrs.

Stanford must also have seen in Dresden, are the only three painters who have consistently been held in high regard from their own lifetimes forward; all other fine artists have at one time or another been affected by the ups and downs of changing taste. During these travels, Mrs. Stanford was coming into her own as a collector. If Leland Stanford was the one who assembled the group of American paintings in the 1870s, clearly Jane was the partner who not only bought Old Master paintings, but also encouraged young Leland to take a serious interest in the arts.

In regard to Leland's education, it was during this winter, on a visit to the south of France, that she made the acquaintance of a young man who was to become important to her household, Herbert C. Nash (50). "I have a tutor in view," she wrote to her husband, "a teacher in the Anglo-American college at Nice. He speaks French well and teaches English to the boys."[24] She interviewed him twice, and then took him on a trial basis. Nash had been born in Nice twenty-four years earlier to an Anglican priest and his wife; his father had established a school there, which Nash had attended.

49 *Woodward's Gardens, a San Francisco gallery and popular pleasure resort, may have been the source of the Stanfords' copy of Raphael's* Madonna of the Chair. *Photograph by Eadweard Muybridge, 1868.* (SM)

50 *Herbert C. Nash with Leland Stanford Junior and two Lathrop cousins in New York in 1882.*

51 *Antonio Bernieri's replica of the marble* Angel of Grief, *1899, by William Wetmore Story.*

52 *Waldo Story, marble relief, 1881.* (Private collection)

his departure, she wrote that she had been taken to see some fine paintings for sale from a family estate, two Van Dycks and a Teniers. "Of course," she told him, "I could not be induced to make purchases of this kind but I wished that you had been with me to have known what you would have done."[26] Five months later, she wrote to him from Italy about several purchases: some small paintings of Naples, some photographs, and a bronze copy of the Farnese Bull that she had bought after seeing the marble original of the large sculptural group, which impressed her greatly.[27]

In Rome a week later, she purchased at young Leland's urging sculptures of the Four Seasons from Antonio Bottinelli, an established Roman artist. "You will be charmed with them," she assured her husband, telling him also of their son's enthusiastic response to the trip. In Rome he had visited the Palace of the Caesars in the forum on a day that found her ill. She explained to her absent husband that

Leland was going to take me himself . . . so that he could leave out that part he thought was too hard for me and show me the frescoes of Livia's room and the golden house of Nero. He has it all at his tongue's end. You will be surprised how much this trip has done for him. I feel very proud of him; he is wonderfully bright, far beyond his years. . . . He is called the little "Augustus" here by the artists, for his head is so much like the bust of Augustus, and he had been to nearly all their studios, and I find he has quite an acquaintance among them.[28]

It was at this time that Jane commissioned Waldo Story, son of the famous American sculptor William Wetmore Story, to make two Neoclassical marble relief sculptures (52). Years later, when her brother died in 1899, Mrs. Stanford ordered as a memorial a replica of W. W. Story's *Angel of Grief,* 1895, the beautiful monument to Emelyn Story in the Protestant Cemetery in Rome, which she had seen in a photograph. Her commission went to Antonio Bernieri, who fabricated the monument in Carrara, giving it a marble canopy (51). Erected near the family mausoleum on the Stanford campus in 1901, the

Educated also in England and in the Collège de France, Nash remained with the Stanfords after the death of his pupil, becoming secretary first to Stanford while he served in the U.S. Senate and later to his widow. Subsequently, he served as secretary to the University's board of trustees, ending his career as University Librarian. It is largely from Nash's pen that we have accounts of young Leland's "little museum" and of the early days of the Leland Stanford Junior Museum.[25]

Jane Stanford's growing independence as a collector can be traced in the letters she sent to her husband over their ten-month separation. From Antwerp, soon after sculpture was damaged in the earthquake and the canopy destroyed. Bernieri replaced the original with a second *Angel* of the same design, but without a canopy. In 1908, it was put in place at Stanford, where it remains.

Another American sculptor on the Via Margutta whom Mrs. Stanford and Leland came to know was Randolph Rogers, whose work was prominently in evidence in northern California. Mrs. E. B. Crocker owned *Nydia, the Blind Girl of Pompeii,* 1855, and the Milton S. Latham collection (Menlo Park) included both *Nydia* and Rogers's *Indian Fisher Girl,* 1866. Mrs. Stanford had Rogers execute both a marble bust and a standing full-length portrait of her son, but these were destroyed on Nob Hill in 1906, together with portraits of Henry Clay, George Washington (after Houdon), and

54 *Rossetti's* Fountain of Love, *photographed by Muybridge in the Nob Hill house, 1878.*

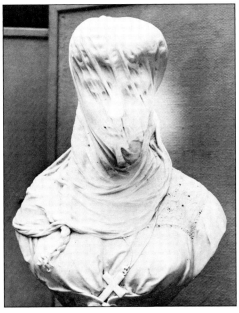

53 *Giovanni Ciniselli,* Modesty, *c. 1881, photographed at Stanford in the 1940s by Clarence John Laughlin.* (SM 85.46)

William H. Seward that she had also bought in 1881 from the artist's studio.

Mrs. Stanford also acquired sculptures by Hiram Powers and Joseph Mozier, though it is not clear where she bought them. By 1882, Powers's *Fisher Boy,* 1848, "nude except for a band of drapery about the loins,"[29] stood at the left of the entrance to the art gallery opposite Mozier's *Forgiven Peri.* Mozier's subject was taken from Thomas Moore's poem *Lalla Rookh,* in which Peri re-

entered Paradise by bringing to God the gifts he most desired, the tears of a repentant old man.

But by far the greater number of the Stanfords' sculptures were by contemporary Italians. According to a report about the Nob Hill house that appeared in the *Cincinnati Commercial* on October 2, 1881, these had been acquired at the Philadelphia Centennial: "The fine collection of Italian sculpture was bought almost in its entirety for the gallery and halls of Governor Stanford's home." Among the works described were four marble pieces by Giovanni Maria Benzoni (1809–1873), a sculptor who by mid-century had established a considerable reputation for himself as a sculptor in marble. His *Diana* and *Apollo* can be seen in Muybridge's photographs of the Nob Hill house in 1878. The Stanfords also owned a Benzoni marble of a girl pulling a thorn from a boy's foot and its companion piece, a dog killing a serpent about to sting his sleeping mistress. Similar in style was *Boy with Bird's Nest* by Pietro Calvi (1833–1884), better known as Calvi of Milan. Still at Stanford is a stone head rendered as if covered by a veil, *Modesty,* by Giovanni Ciniselli (1832–1883), exemplifying a type of sculptural *tour de force* very much in evidence during the 1880s (53). Also by Ciniselli were the figures of *Morning,* "a woman with flowers in her arms and a child at her feet," and *Night,* "a torchbearer with an owl." In addition, the Stanfords owned *Susanna* by Giovanni Battista Lombardi (1823–1880) and a marble *Fountain of Love* by Antonio Rossetti (born in 1819), which was highly prized by Mrs. Stanford. It, too, can be seen in a Muybridge photograph (54). (At the Centennial, Rossetti made a name for himself with two allegorical figures, the *Genius of Electricity* and the *Genius of Steam.*) Of interest, too, was the group *Lincoln and the Slave,* 1867, by Pasquale Romanelli

(c. 1812–1887) which appears to have been the same sculpture placed by W. D. Howells in the Laphams' parlor, though Howells did not specify the artist by name: "A white marble group of several figures, expressing an Italian conception of Lincoln Freeing the Slaves,— a Latin negro and his wife,—with our Eagle flapping his wings in approval, at Lincoln's feet."[30]

Early in April 1881, Mrs. Stanford bought from a "noble family near Florence" the group of Italian Old Masters, since destroyed, that were alluded to in the *San Francisco Chronicle,* May 14, 1882, the date the paintings were first shown in San Francisco. "There are probably few, if any, private collections in the country that can show so many genuine specimens of the Old Masters as are here gathered." The journalist, evidently aware of the frustrating problem of authentication, went on the explain: "The numberless frauds styled 'Old Masters,' that have been imposed on a not very well informed public in matters artistic, attest to the care which is to be used in making selections from even the choicest of European galleries." Although it is not known if anyone advised Mrs. Stanford in making her selections, or for that matter their precise source, the taste implied by the group is a decidedly English one, old-fashioned though it was for the 1880s.

The earliest work among Mrs. Stanford's selections was a *Madonna and Child* attributed to Francesco Francia (1450–1517), an artist in the Circle of Raphael whose work was very much in demand during the mid-nineteenth century. "No specimens of art of the period," the *Chronicle* announced, "are thought to surpass those of Francia." As Francis Haskell observed in *Rediscoveries in Art* (1976), the choice of Francia was a kind of compromise for those in England who disdained the Pre-Raphaelites.[31] Another painting in the Stanford group that fell into this category was a *Madonna of the Flowers* by Gaudenzio Ferrera (1484–1546). From the Venetian sixteenth century came a Veronese (figure of *Hope*) and a *Masquerade,* attributed to Titian's student Paris Bordone (1500–1571) and described as a "single figure of a woman in a masquerading costume."[32]

Among the Italian Baroque paintings in the group were works attributed to artists who had been held in high regard by English connoisseurs since the eighteenth century but who, by Mrs. Stanford's day, were beginning to lose ground: the Bolognese Guido Reni, Francesco Albano, Donato Creti, and Domenichino; the Florentines Giovanni Biliverti, Francesco Furini, Carlo Dolci; the Neapolitan Salvator Rosa; and from Ferrara, Guercino, whose painting *Flora's Toilet* was "unusually pleas-ing and imaginative . . . the goddess is attended by two cupids, one of whom is placing a wreath on her head, while the other holds a mirror to reflect her beauties." Mrs. Stanford seems to have been transfixed by Cupid and Venus, motifs that run through eight of the pictures. The two paintings attributed to Reni were *Cupid,* "a simple figure of the boy with the implements of his trade," and *Innocence Disarming Cupid.* Guido's student, Giacomo Sementi, provided *Venus and Endymion,* a subject repeated in the Furini. Three paintings by Albano were entitled *Dance of Angels around the Statues of Venus and Cupid, Nymphs and Cupids,* and *King David,* 'encircled by a group of winged boys, presumably cupids, who may be possibly intended to suggest his amorous tendencies." The last of this motif was seen in Giovanni Battista Tiepolo's *Cupid Guiding Hope.* (The eighteenth-century Venetian painter Tiepolo had become popular in the 1870s after his "discovery" by Delacroix and the publication of a sympathetic study by Charles Blanc in 1876.)

Another classical subject was Creti's *Rest of Diana after the Chase.* What remained was Christian in content: *Prayer for Peace* by Elisabetta Sirani, the *Finding of Moses* by Biliverti, *Rebecca and Eleazar at the Well* by Cagliare, and two canvases by Carlo Dolci, *Innocence* (a woman holding a lamb) and a Madonna; according to the *Chronicle,* the Madonna had "more admirers, or perhaps it may be said, worshippers, than any other simple head of Madonna ever painted." And at some time during the year, Jane Stanford acquired a portrait of the Princess Labella ascribed to Greuze and the monumental *Resurrection* by Benjamin West (55), the only one of the group that found its way to the Museum, where it remains.

In the general make-up of the art collection the Stanfords assembled for their home before the death of their son in 1884, Old Master paintings accounted for less than a sixth of the total. By far the greater number were works by contemporary artists, proportions that hold true for the majority of collections assembled with the great industrial fortunes of the Gilded Age. Indeed, as Gerard Reitlinger points out in *The Economics of Taste* (1961), the years from 1860 to 1914 constituted the golden age of living painters. One of the reasons for the surge of interest in contemporary art on the part of Americans newly rich after the Civil War was undoubtedly a fear of the fraud and inexperience that caused so-called Old Masters to be discounted as inauthentic by

55 *Benjamin West,* The Resurrection, *oil on canvas.* (SM 12024)

connoisseurs and art historians like Bernard Berenson, who were making it their business in the 1880s and 1890s to establish standards of judgment. In the drawing collection of Cornelius Vanderbilt, for example, of the nine Michelangelos, two Raphaels, eleven Titians, twelve Tintorettos, nine Rembrandts, and two Leonardos acquired in Florence in the 1870s, none turned out to be accepted by later specialists.[33] (Of course, credibility for the Stanfords' Old Masters is moot, since none remains to be examined.) How much more reassuring for unseasoned patrons to be able to go to an artist's studio and watch him at his work, as Stanford had been able to watch Thomas Hill in San Francisco. Indeed, from all that is known of the aesthetic quality of the Stanfords' collection, the American paintings were the finest portion. And this is very likely due to the guidance the family received from Bierstadt.

Overall, works by living foreign artists had a slight edge over native stock in the Stanfords' house, as they did in other mansions of the era, since the late-nineteenth century was seeing the breakdown of the traditional association of artist and patron. Instead of having a Bierstadt with them in Europe, the Stanfords were guided by a market system managed by an art establishment into which forces other than inherent artistic value had entered, forces made complex by a variety of factors. Prominent among these was the need to sort out the worth of the two hundred thousand paintings being produced each decade in Paris alone in order to find buyers for them among the rising middle class with its innate preference for the anecdotal, sentimental, and realistic style that conveyed a "you-are-there" kind of verism. Never before had France had so many professional painters—artists, that is, who earned their living solely by painting. In the words of Emile Zola, Paris had become a purveyor to the world not only of soap, gloves, and fine attire, but of fine art as well.[34] Zola couldn't decide if the public's taste for trivia was inculcated by the painters or demanded of them by the crowd. In any case, in all of Europe, art's most popular outlet was the Official Exposition of Living Artists, the Paris Salon.

Arriving from Italy in time to attend the opening of the Salon on May 1, 1881, Mrs. Stanford and her son joined the crowds in the Palace of Industry on the Champs Elysées, where 2,500 exhibits were on view. "It offers a fine sight," young Leland noted in his journal.[35] But after four hours, he had had enough, and when his mother went to the Bois with some friends, he headed for the stamp *bourse,* bought some "good ones," and followed his purchases with a ride on the carrousel.

Before they returned to the States in December 1882, the Stanfords had acquired paintings by numerous Salon painters—among them, Bouguereau, Gérôme, Gisbert, Toulmouche, and Worms—and by their peers in Austria (Humborg), Belgium (Col, de Haas, Markelbach,

56 Meissonier painted this portrait of Leland Stanford in Paris during four weeks in the summer of 1881. (SM 12038)

Verboeckhoven), Holland (Kaemmerer, Portielje), and Germany (Knaus, Meyer von Bremen, Schenk). When Governor Stanford joined his wife and son in June, he had his portrait painted by the most admired artist of all, Meissonier (56), whose photographic realism made him enormously popular with middle-class buyers willing to pay enormous prices for his work. Then in the fall, Jane Stanford was portrayed by the celebrated portraitist Léon Bonnat (57), and Leland Stanford Junior, by Carolus-Duran (58 and cover), the friend of Manet and teacher of Sargent.[36] In the spring of 1882, when the *Catalogue of Leland Stanford's Collection of Pictures* was published, the Collection totaled 181.

57 Léon Bonnat, Jane Stanford,
1881, oil on canvas. (SM 12020)

44

W HEN HE WAS fifteen, Leland Stanford Junior returned to Europe with his family for a second time. While at home in the meantime, he had added the souvenirs of his first trip to his boyish treasures and arranged his collection in a little museum on the third floor of the Nob Hill house. His Cabinet of Curiosities included stuffed birds from California, minerals from Nevada, Indian pottery from the Southwest, soldiers' gear from the Franco-Prussian War, a Persian helmet inlaid with gold, a cannon ball thrown at Fort Sumter—all catalogued and displayed with the help of his mother.

Now, on his second trip, the boy grew more serious in his goals. He had spent the winter of the intervening year in New York, where his parents, anticipating their son's attendance at Harvard, had taken the Lorillard mansion at 479 Fifth Avenue. The boy became interested in archaeology, an interest fostered by his study of the Cesnola collection of Cypriot antiquities at the Metropolitan Museum. His father had made a gift of $1,000 to the Museum, and no doubt this encouraged Luigi Palma di Cesnola—its director and the excavator of the collection—to take an interest in the young man.

Cesnola's rise from a somewhat impoverished youth as a soldier in the army of Sardinia to the directorship of the Metropolitan Museum was an interesting one, well told by Calvin Tomkins in his account of the Metropolitan, *Merchants and Masterpieces* (1970). Cesnola had assembled his huge collection from excavations he had conducted while holding the post of U.S. consul on Cyprus from 1865 to 1876, an appointment awarded him after service in the American Civil War. He had taken 35,573 objects from the sites of 16 ancient cities, 15 temples, 65 necropoli, and 60,332 tombs. Like other nineteenth-century amateurs—like Schliemann, for example, with whom he was often compared—Cesnola believed that the plunder belonged to him. After negotiations for the sale of his collection to the Hermitage, the Louvre, and the British Museum had broken down, Cesnola succeeded when the Metropolitan bought it for $50,000. Its president, John Taylor Johnston, praised the material as "the most precious single discovery of ancient art ever made."[37] Opportunistically, Cesnola was able to sell himself with the collection.

58 Carolus-Duran, Leland Stanford Junior, 1881, oil on canvas. (SM 12002)

In Europe, with letters of introduction from Cesnola, Leland pursued the archaeological researches he had begun in New York "with more fervor than ever," his tutor later wrote.[38] In search of artifacts to add to his cabinet, he made the rounds with Herbert Nash of the public auction rooms in Paris and of well-known art and antiquities dealers like Rollin Feuardent and Jean Henri Hoffmann. Hoffmann, born in Hamburg in 1823, had assembled a collection of particular strength in Egyptian antiquities, part of which was acquired by the Louvre in 1886 and part in 1895. Leland bought from Hoffmann a bronze of the god Osiris, as well as bronze cats of various sizes, a figure of Apis, the sacred bull, hawks, serpents, two ibises, a crocodile, and several figures of the gods Horus, Osiris, and Anubis. "Some may wonder at these tastes in one so young," his tutor Nash reminisced, "but, besides being developed by education, their existence was in great measure due to his natural desire to trace things to their source."[39]

This search for origins provided the impetus for much nineteenth-century inquiry and sparked the great studies in archaeology, ethnography, cultural anthropology, religion, and orientalism to which the youngster was responding with his adolescent passion for Egyptology. It was a passion shared by such contemporaries as Albert Lythgoe, the American Egyptologist born in 1868 and educated at Harvard, who served as curator of Egyptian art at the Metropolitan from 1906 to 1929, and George Reisner, Harvard-trained, who excavated in Egypt for many years, particularly at Giza, and served as curator of the Egyptian department in the Boston Museum from 1910 and then as professor of Egyptology at Harvard.

For Leland, in Paris in September 1883, the future held seven months during which, as Nash put it, "his labors for his museum were the recreations of his leisure moments."[40] Egypt had been his great interest ever since the Rosetta Stone had awakened his curiosity. Dating from 196 B.C. and discovered in 1799, the Rosetta Stone provided the clues that led to the decipherment of hieroglyphic writing accomplished ultimately by Jean François Champollion (1790–1832) in France. For the nineteenth century, the Rosetta Stone became something of a sacred object: the key to discovery of a lost chapter in the history of mankind. At the Louvre the boy copied hieroglyphs from sarcophagi and scarabs, spending the evenings deciphering their meaning and also studying Champollion's accounts of Egypt (59, 60). (Leland was able to acquire a large alabaster jar that had been brought to France by one of Champollion's assistants.) His success in deciphering hieroglyphs was aided by the attention of

59 *The hieroglyphs on the canopic jar deciphered in Leland Junior's hand.* (SM 17196 bis)

60 *Egyptian alabaster canopic jar with head of Kebehsenuef.* (SM 17196)

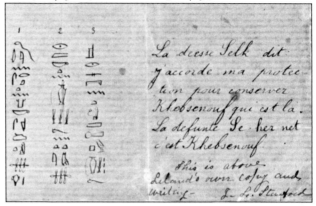

61 *Inscribed column fragment from the Sanctuary of Eleusis.* (SM 17488)

Georges Daressy, four years his senior, and another of the generation of budding Egyptologists. In 1887 Daressy became assistant keeper of the Bulak Museum in Cairo and, under the directorship of the great Gaston Maspero, served as secretary to the Service des Antiquités.

Journeying to ancient sites in Italy and Greece with his parents in the winter of 1883, Leland turned his attention to classical art, writing to an aunt that he was expecting "to get a good many things for my Museum. I only make a collection of Egyptian, Greek, and Roman."[41] Like other tourists of the time, he was able to pick up objects on the site to bring home as souvenirs. At the Sanctuary of Eleusis near Athens, for example, he found a fragment of a column capital (61) and an inscribed

47

62 *Mosaic table top acquired from the Stanfords in 1881. Views of Rome surround the Capitoline* *Doves of Pliny, the popular mosaic preserved from antiquity.* (SM 85.77)

relief treating rituals sacred to Demeter and Persephone. From the Tomb of Cecilia Metella on the Via Appia outside the walls of Rome came another relief. A mosaic fragment from Pompeii may have come from his earlier visit in 1881, when his mother read to him about Vesuvius and the last days of Pompeii and he was "wild with interest." Jane Stanford, too, was seized by the romance of the ancient site. "I felt almost transported into another world," she had written to her husband; "this is so grand, so solemn, the streets still beautifully paved with large square blocks of stone that show the wear of wheels. . . . I could not sleep that night I was walking through deserted streets and the picture would not leave my brain."[42]

Then, in Athens in January 1884, the greatest thrill of all: a visit to Heinrich Schliemann, the extraordinary amateur who revolutionized scholarship by his discoveries in the world of Aegean prehistory, including the Great Treasure of Troy in 1873 and the Gold of Mycenae in 1876. Schliemann made Leland a present of some "fetishes or charms" he had found in the Troad, taking them from a case in his museum and explaining that the little earthenware nuts with holes bored through their centers were a species of penates, "nailed up against the walls of private houses as household Gods, to whom sacrifice of prayer could be made."[43] (Actually, the beads

are weights and spinning whorls.) Schliemann invited the Stanfords and Nash to accompany him the next day to Marathon, the famous field where the Greeks defeated the Persians in 490 B.C. But the family's schedule left them no time for this.[44]

Born in Germany but an American citizen, Schliemann was a millionaire like Stanford. He had made his fortune as a commodities broker in Amsterdam and St. Petersburg before dedicating his considerable energies to Homeric excavation. Remarkably, he had made a trip to Sacramento in 1851 in search of gold, a year's adventure that he must have enjoyed recounting to the Californians when he was their host in Greece more than thirty years later. As Leo Deuel has remarked in his edition of Schliemann's memoirs, the man was in many ways "the new *Homo americanus* who rose from dismal poverty, and made several fortunes (none of which he lost), yet cultivated sobriety, parsimony, clean living, long working hours, self-discipline, determination, and fellowship."[45] Controversy surrounded both his finds and his methods; yet he inspired a new breed of modern archaeologists. Indeed, as the literary critic Hugh Kenner wrote in his study of Ezra Pound (1971), Schliemann exerted a seminal influence on the whole spectrum of modern thought. Not surprisingly, years later, when Jane Stanford was putting the finishing touches on the memorial Museum, she determined to have a monumental figure of the seated Schliemann on the entrance steps. Entering into correspondence with Schliemann's widow in 1891, the year of his death, Mrs. Stanford had photographs of the man sent to an American sculptor she had come to know in Florence, William Couper. She requested an estimate for a figure of heroic size, but apparently the fee was high, and the project was abandoned.[46]

By early February 1884, the Stanfords were in Naples, and young Leland wrote to a friend at home that he had had a very nice time with Dr. Schliemann and his wife. "I bought a good many antiquities for my museum and Papa gave me 4000 francs for its support."[47] Some were purchased on the Acropolis; others, like the two Tanagra figurines of a sleeping woman and a woman suckling a baby, were bought from a Dr. Lambros in Athens. Leland told, too, of his trip to Constantinople, where the Sultan's aide-de-camp showed him diamonds by the bushel and an emerald "as large as your hand"; and how Nash had lost his valise crossing the Danube "and now anything that can't be found happened to be in that." But he said that he'd been going it too hard and wasn't feeling well. A month later, in Florence, Leland Stanford Junior was dead of typhoid fever.

The Leland Stanford Junior Museum
'. . . a great many rare and unique articles.'

T̶HE IDEA OF founding a museum in memory of their son loomed large in the Stanfords' minds during the months that followed the boy's death. Immediately upon reaching New York from Europe in May 1884, with young Leland's body, which was to be interred in California, Governor Stanford wrote to Luigi Cesnola; he wanted to buy duplicates of the Metropolitan's Cypriot antiquities for the museum he was founding in California.[1] Within days, the Metropolitan's trustees agreed to the request, and Cesnola soon selected about five thousand objects for which Stanford paid $10,000.[2] But by June the Stanfords were discussing the museum and two other projects with educators at Cornell, Yale, Harvard, Johns Hopkins, and the Massachusetts Institute of Technology. President Charles Eliot of Harvard later recalled that they had not yet decided when they saw him about "the nature of the monument." They discussed several possibilities:

One was a university to be placed in Palo Alto as near as possible to a tree under which their son had once eaten luncheon. Another was a large institution to be situated in San Francisco and to combine a museum with a large hall in which free public lectures in considerable variety should be given. The third was a technical school. . . .[3]

Eliot advised them that the most desirable of the trio was a university, but he was left with the impression that Leland Stanford actually had more than one object in view: "He wanted to build a monument to his dead boy; but he also wanted to do something that would interest his wife for the rest of her life and give her solid satisfaction." Eliot felt that the latter motive was actually the strongest and, interestingly, that Mrs. Stanford "had done more thinking on the subject" than her husband.

Although the Stanfords included the Museum in the University's founding grant of November 11, 1885, two years later they still spoke of building it in San Francisco. David Starr Jordan, the University's first president, later explained that the Stanfords had initially wanted to carry out their son's wish to form a great collection for the city of San Francisco, but eventually this idea "did not satisfy them as being sufficiently generous."[4] Thus, the Museum, originally planned as an independent institution, was ultimately merged with the University. But it remained in Mrs. Stanford's mind more intimately identified with the memory of her child, whose boyhood collecting it was to continue on a monumental scale. As Paul Turner explains in the essay that follows, the Museum's huge building was given both a location separate from the main body of the University buildings and a distinctive architectural form borrowed from that of the Athens National Museum. Its Neoclassical design set it apart from the University's master plan for a Romanesque-Mission style designed by the landscape architect Frederick Law Olmstead and by the architectural associates and successors of H. H. Richardson, who died in 1886, Shepley, Rutan, and Coolidge. When the Museum was inaugurated, on the University's opening day in 1891, it was only the fifth university museum of any size to have been built in the century, following those of Yale (1832), Oxford (1845), Cambridge (1848), and Princeton (1887). But in Mrs. Stanford's mind it was to be, like the Metropolitan Museum of Art in New York, commensurate with the great museums of Europe that she had visited with her son.

From the Metropolitan's holdings were to come most of the archaeological additions to Leland Stanford Junior's collection (63).[5] Dating from the Bronze Age to Roman

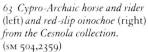

63 Cypro-Archaic horse and rider (left) and red-slip oinochoe (right) from the Cesnola collection. (SM 504,2359)

times, all had been excavated or bought on the island of Cyprus by Cesnola during his years there as U.S. consul. (See pp. 124–127 for an illustrated description of the Cesnola collection at Stanford.) Cesnola had sold the collection to the Metropolitan, and, making himself indispensable to its cataloguing and installation, he had become the museum's first director.

In New York, Cesnola's most stalwart supporter was John Taylor Johnston, the Metropolitan's first president. Like Stanford, Johnston was a collector of European and American paintings. Both men, moreover, were railroad men. Johnston, a New Yorker by birth with a law degree from Yale, was president for thirty years of both the Lehigh and Susquehanna and the Central of New Jersey. His successor, Henry Gurdon Marquand, another New York art patron of the 1870s and 1880s, was also a railroad executive. In 1874, he bought the St. Louis Iron Mountain and the Southern Railroad, which he ran successfully until 1882, when Jay Gould bought him out. Like Stanford and Johnston, Marquand owned a large number of Salon paintings. But he also owned thirty-seven Old Masters, which he placed on loan to the Metropolitan in 1888 and later bequeathed, a gift that included two works by Rembrandt and one by Vermeer. Acquisitions at the Metropolitan were scarce until the turn of the century, but with this gift came the beginnings of the shift to the masterpieces associated ever since with New York. In similar fashion, the president of the Central Pacific Railroad and his wife bequeathed their collection of twenty-two Old Master paintings, which included a Veronese and a Domenichino, to Stanford. Farfetched as it may seem now to compare the two institutions, in the formative decades of the 1880s and 1890s it was not so.

When the Metropolitan's first Central Park building was inaugurated in 1880, one-quarter of its gallery space was given over to the Cypriot antiquities (64). Young Leland had seen the newly installed collection when he visited the Museum during the winter of 1882 and expressed to Cesnola his interest in the "art-education" of the American people. The Stanfords, too, wished to open *their* museum with the Cesnola antiquities in place. But they were willing to leave their purchases (of 1884) in crates at the Metropolitan until they had a building in which to display them.[6] When the Stanford Museum was first opened to visitors in the fall of 1893, two years after the University had opened, the Cesnola collection occupied roughly a tenth of the gallery space (65). It was Mrs. Stanford's wish that Stanford students make use of the entire collection in conjunction with lectures given by Walter Miller, Stanford's first professor of Latin and Archaeology.

50

64 *The Cesnola collection installed at the Metropolitan Museum in 1882 when Leland Stanford Junior saw it.*

B Y THEN Mrs. Stanford had supplemented Cesnola's findings with twenty-one Greek vases (67), terracottas, and bronzes acquired in Paris from Athanasios S. Rhousopoulos. Professor of archaeology and philology at the National University in Athens and a member of the Archaeological Society in Athens as early as 1860, Rhousopoulos had a large number of scholarly publications to his credit. And for Mrs. Stanford he provided a descriptive catalogue of the objects he had sold her.[7] Among them was an archaic terracotta protome of a woman's face (66) found on the island of Chalke near Rhodes. Writing that "with the exception of the British Museum, no other Museum of Europe" owned a similar mask, Rhousopoulos pointed out that its "closed mouth with its laughing expression" would "render it of great interest to students of Ancient Art." An Attic red figure hydria had come from a tomb south of Athens at Pikrodaphne excavated in 1863. A bronze Hekate found in Gytheion in Lakonia provided an unusual sculptural variant of the goddess' image:

Over her three heads she has a basket-shaped ornament, decorated

66 Terracotta protome, early fifth century B.C., purchased by Jane Stanford in 1888 for the Leland Stanford Junior Collection. (SM 17438)

67 Attic red-figure pelike, c. 470 B.C., acquired from Rhousopoulos in Paris. (SM 17410)

51

with six snakes tied together in pairs. But their heads are those of cocks instead of snakes. This is a rarely found combination of the symbols of watchfulness and fear. Very interesting also are the four stars with eight rays each, symbolic of the goddess of Night.[8]

Rhousopoulos also described an idol made of solid

65 The Cesnola collection installed at Stanford in 1893 by the Museum's founder.

bronze, a satyr from Ligourio, for which he claimed an origin of the eighth century B.C., making the point that since it showed no similarity to Egyptian bronze work, the piece proved the originality of Greek bronze style.

Director of the Museum in all but title, Jane Stanford had embarked on her new career at the age of fifty-six; by 1893, when the Museum opened, she had added more than fifteen thousand objects to her son's collection. But at the heart of the Museum were two rooms set apart as special memorials. Both were replicas of rooms at home where Leland Stanford Junior had kept his "International Museum" (68).[9] At Stanford, one of these rooms contained Leland's own arrangement of materials acquired before 1882, and the other, the purchases he had made abroad during 1883 and 1884, together with mementos of his boyhood, including portraits, added by his parents.[10] It was Mrs. Stanford's wish that these two rooms remain always as she had arranged them, and at first she kept them locked; they were private spaces to which she often came either alone or with her closest friends. She said repeatedly that the University was founded on her son's collections—they were the "connecting link" between him and the school.[11]

According to Nash's account of the Museum's origin, high on the list of desiderata of Leland Stanford Junior at the time of his death were Chinese and Japanese art objects as well as American Indian artifacts. Thus, one of his mother's early major purchases was a remarkable collection of specimens spanning the entire prehistory of the American Midwest. Assembled by William McAdams in the early 1880s chiefly in Missouri, Kansas, and Illinois, it included the famous archaeological finds at Cahokia. Authenticated by the director of the U.S. Bureau of Ethnology, the collection was bought by Mrs. Stanford from the New Orleans Exposition of 1884–85. (Subsequently, McAdams prepared the archaeological exhibition for the State of Illinois at the World-Columbian Exposition.) By 1886, Mrs. Stanford had added a few examples of American Indian pottery (69) and basketry of the Southwest together with Alaskan artifacts and mortars and pestles unearthed near Palo Alto. By the time the Museum opened, she had substantially expanded the American Indian holdings, particularly in the area of Northwest Coast material (70). The Haida carved-argillite totems at Stanford are outstanding for their size and the intricacy of their carving (71).[12]

An opportunity to fulfill young Leland's desire for Asian acquisitions presented itself shortly after the Stanfords moved to Washington in 1885 at the beginning of Leland Stanford's first term in the Senate. Mrs. Stanford

68 Egyptian objects and Gallo-Roman remains, including a piling from the bed of the Rhine near Coblenz, from the collection formed by Leland Stanford Junior when he was fifteen.

was able to acquire a group of 289 Japanese objects that had been assembled by Charles E. DeLong, U.S. minister to Japan from 1869 to 1873, during the presidency of Ulysses S. Grant. Consisting mainly of armor and weapons, his collection also included musical instruments—"a ladie's banjo"—cloisonné vases, lacquers (72), kimonos, and eighty-two watercolors. (The watercolors have long been missing from the collection, and most of the other things have been sold.) Not long after, a second collection formed contemporaneously in Japan was given to the Museum by the sister of Eugene M. Van Reed, Queen Victoria's consul general to Japan from 1866 to 1873. This group of "curios" included an album of 187 privately commissioned color woodblock prints called *surimono*, or New Year's greeting cards. Dating from 1806 to 1813 and combining pictures and poems, the sheets were the work of such artists and poets as Ryūryūkyo Shinsai and Yomo Utagaki Magao (73).[13] In

52

69 *New Mexico, Zuni water jar.* (SM 4451)

70 *Northwest Coast ceremonial helmet.* (SM 8672)

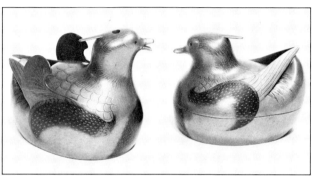

71 (far left) *Queen Charlotte Islands, Haida pole of carved argillite.* (SM 7584)

72 *Gold and black Japanese lacquer, part of a food-service set, from the DeLong collection.* (SM 9808)

73 Woman with a Fan, *1806, by Kitagawa Utamaro I, poem by Yūchōdō Tsuyshige.* (SM 62.86)

at Stanford, *Kitchen Piece,* 1890 (76), with its rabbit, quail, onions, wine crock, and platter, was one of few such kitchen still lifes by an American master of *trompe l'oeil,* although it was a subject much favored by European artists. Four other paintings by Goodwin— *Ducks,*

74 Chinese export American eagle plaque, c. 1820. (SM 16106)

75 Richard LaBarre Goodwin, Cabin Door, *1889, oil on canvas.* (SM 12072)

Washington, too, an unidentified woman presented as a gift to the Museum an American Eagle plaque exported from China, dating from about 1820 and bearing the letters IN GOD WE TRUST (74).

As a side note of architectural interest, when Stanford was chairman of the Senate Committee on Public Buildings the construction of the San Jose Post Office was authorized by Act of Congress on April 28, 1890. Completed five years later, the building was constructed of sandstone from the same quarries that supplied the University's buildings, the Goodrich quarry in Almaden Township and the Stanford quarry south of San Jose.[14] Its form, too, replicated the Romanesque-Mission style of the Stanford campus. Currently, the building houses the San Jose Museum of Art.

The Washington setting also provided new opportunities for acquiring paintings: the Stanfords' stay there coincided with a three-year sojourn by Richard LaBarre Goodwin, an American artist born in Syracuse, New York, who did not remain long in any one place. Popular with the California delegation, Goodwin sold a still life to Senator George Hearst and eight others to Senator Stanford. Among them was *Cabin Door,* 1889 (75), the earliest version of a theme that was to become the artist's trademark over the next twenty years. The painting is dated by the postmark "Dec. 2, '89" in the upper right-hand corner of the *trompe l'oeil* envelope. Both the French stamp and the soft hat are borrowings from William Harnett, as Alfred Frankenstein pointed out in *After the Hunt,* his book on the popular Harnett and his followers.[15] Frankenstein observed, too, that a second Goodwin

76 Richard La Barre Goodwin,
Kitchen Piece, *1890, oil on*
canvas. (SM 12016)

Quail, Trout, and *Essentials of Life*—were sent to the Museum by Mrs. Stanford, but these were sold in the early 1950s.

Contemporary European paintings were added to the Collection during the Stanfords' trips abroad in 1888, 1890, and 1892. As before, landscape and anecdotal scenes of the sort promoted by Samuel Avery were favored, but now acquisitions were almost exclusively by such German Academic painters as Caeser Bimerman, Johan Jungblut, Wilhelm Rögge, Viktor Schivert, and Fritz Werner. An exception was *Liberty Regulated by Law* by the French artist Charles Landelle, a student of Paul Delaroche and Ary Scheffer, who had painted, shortly after young Stanford's death, an allegorical portrait of

Leland and Jane Stanford with their son hovering in the ether above them. When it was first seen in California, the portrait, visible in an old photograph of the Museum's memorial room (77), had added fuel to the fire of speculation about the Stanfords having received messages from the boy through a spiritualist. But the artist insisted that the painting commemorated nothing of the sort; he had simply suggested to the Stanfords that the boy's departure from earth be implied by placing him against a cloudy background.[16]

Residence in Washington, which lasted until the Senator's death in 1893, led also to a close friendship between Jane Stanford and members of the Grant family, particularly Julia Dent Grant, the president's widow.

56

77 *Memorial Room at the turn of the century with Landelle's painting of the three Stanfords. From the Museum's 1903 catalogue:*

"The Memorial Room was designed to contain the mementoes of Senator and Mrs. Stanford. Here are found ancestral portraits of the Stanford and Lathrop families; two cases devoted to the Grant family collection; racing trophies; Muybridge's first photographs of Animals in Motion, *and subsequent works; the* Last Spike, *and other historical relics of the Central Pacific Railroad. To Mrs. Stanford is due the large assortment of beautiful rare lace—Point, Alençon, Chantilly, Duchesse, Honiton, Valenciennes, and others; also rare India shawls, fans, Worth dresses, antique jewelry, and European souvenirs."*

Over the years, the Stanfords were approached several times by the Grants for special favors. Ida Grant, wife of the president's second son, wished in 1884 that a job might be found for her husband in a railroad office.[17] In 1889, when Frederick D. Grant finally found an appointment of another sort—as U.S. minister to Austria-Hungary—his mother sent a telegram expressing both her delight and her "heartfelt thanks" to Leland Stanford.[18] As soon as F. D. Grant and his family were settled in Vienna, the Stanfords, together with Mrs. Stanford's sister Anna Maria and her husband, David Hewes, paid them a visit. After they left, the minister saw to the shipment home of antiques the Stanfords had purchased abroad.[19] It was Julia Grant's hope, moreover, that she might persuade Jane Stanford to buy outright the manuscript of her memoirs, which for one reason or another publishers had rejected.[20] (Mrs. Grant wanted the money to buy the Stanford's Washington house at 1701 K Street, left vacant by the senator's death.) But nothing came of the proposal. Nor did Mrs. Stanford reply favorably to Mrs. Grant's request of 1892 that her third son, Jesse, be given a job in Palo Alto either as librarian at the University or as curator of the Museum.[21]

A portrait of Ulysses S. Grant (78) was among the new acquisitions assembled in the Stanfords' Washington residence, together with furnishings and paintings brought down from the Lorillard mansion, which they had taken a few years before in New York City. The Grant portrait was evidently executed after his death from a photograph taken about 1881, and it was probably commissioned by the Stanfords for their own possession. The artist was a young woman, Georgiana Campbell (1861–1931),[22] who also provided the Stanfords with a portrait of Senator Stanford in 1890, as well as six other portraits of men of consequence. All were members of the University's first board of trustees. They were Josiah Stanford, Leland's brother; Henry Ashburner; John Franklin Miller (79), U.S. senator from California from 1880 to 1886; Lorenzo Sawyer, appointed by Grant in 1869 as U.S. circuit judge for the Ninth Circuit, and the first president of the University's board of trustees; William Morris Stewart (80), U.S. senator from Nevada; and Henry Vrooman. All of the portraits, in matching frames, appear to have been painted from photographs. But a sculpted bust of Jane Stanford's sister Anna Maria, 1888, which subsequently entered the Museum's Collection, was executed from life by Gaetano Trentanove (1858–1937), an Italian-born sculptor well-known for the marble statues of American patriots that dotted the corridors of the Capitol.

78 Ulysses S. Grant. (SM 12067)

57

79 John Franklin Miller. (SM 62.289)

80 William Morris Stewart. (SM 63.87)

The Stanford Family Sculpture

In Florence in 1890, Mrs. Stanford opened negotiations with two American sculptors working there for a commemorative family group to be executed in marble. One was William Couper; the other, Larkin Mead. Both were accomplished artists with numerous commissions to their credit. Deliberation over the choice of artist continued for the better part of two years; and even after the selection was made, years passed before Mrs. Stanford decided in favor of bronze as the medium instead of marble. Couper had a decided advantage: years before, he had been called to the deathbed of Leland Stanford Junior for the purpose of taking a cast of the bust and head. After the cast was seen by the Stanfords, Couper wrote on August 12, 1890, that Mrs. Stanford's remarks about the bust pleased him.

[They] amply compensate me for all I went through when I saw you and the Governor in the most trying moments of your affliction . . . Having the materials to make a statue of your son, (excepting the exact height) there is no reason I could not give you an entirely satisfactory portrait. . . . When you have fully determined about the family group, I would be pleased to make sketches and subject them to your approval.[23]

Meanwhile, he set to work on an order for two marble sphinxes to be placed at the entrance to the family mausoleum on the Stanford campus.[24] These were completed a year later (81). In the interim Mrs. Stanford approached Couper about two other sculptural commissions: one was a statue of Heinrich Schliemann to be placed on the Museum's front steps; and the other was a request for the recommendation of a "cheap sculptor" to provide standing figures for the Museum's parapet. Couper's reply to the second request was sharply phrased:

Now as to the cheap sculptor: I am obliged to say I do not know any one whom I could take the responsibility of recommending even at a much higher figure than you mention, for cheap work means bad work naturally, and when you see bad work of an artistic nature on your Art Museum, further expense would simply be involved in removing it and having better put in its place.[25]

While Couper attempted to set Mrs. Stanford straight about the importance of quality in art, Larkin Mead was already in correspondence with her about the family group. Indeed, by December 26, 1890, Mead had completed clay models (82). He recommended that figures of such grand proportions—Governor Stanford was to be seven feet tall—be cut of Serravezza marble, of which she could see examples in the statues of Jefferson and Franklin in the Senate building. The Stanford group would be taller, Mead continued, than the figures of Columbus and Isabella that he had made for the Sacra-

81 The Stanford Family mausoleum with the Couper sphinxes, c. 1900.

mento Capitol, and which D. O. Mills had given to the State of California at a cost of $15,000 paid to Mead. Despite the larger proportions of the Stanford group, Mead would charge less for the work: $8,000. Mrs. Stanford had only to telegraph the word "commence," and he would set out at once to find the block of marble. He also made a point of saying that he would be glad to make any changes that she might suggest.[26]

Despite this progress, Couper was still in the running five months later. In May 1891, he wrote that he would be pleased to undertake the family group.[27] He said that he had carefully preserved the molds and models of young Leland's bust and head and that he would use them in fashioning the new piece. He envisioned Governor and Mrs. Stanford seated in two handsome chairs with their son stepping between them. The work would take three years to cut from one block of marble and the cost would be $22,000. In November 1891, he again wrote to Mrs. Stanford from Florence, saying that he would "not only be greatly pleased to undertake the work," but that he would put his whole heart into it and give her the benefit of his best efforts. He reminded her that the molds from Leland's bust and head would be of "infinite value in constructing his statue."[28]

There the matter lay until 1894, when Mead, in a letter of condolence on the death of Senator Stanford, prompted his widow to think again of the work.

The death of good Senator Stanford was a serious loss to our America. Senator Stanford, Mr. W. Corcoran of Washington and Mr. Childs of Philadelphia were the trio of American philanthropists, and now Mr. Childs is the only one left. I was proud as an American to read the encomiums and rare praise of Senator Stanford in the European papers at the time of his death. His name coupled with your own and of the dear boy will be as household words for centuries to come. I wish to say a word about the Family Group. My part of the work was done years ago. (That is the creation in clay.) All that is now to be done is to employ the *best* workmen to reproduce my model in marble. Whenever you decide to have the workmen commence the group in marble please write me and I will see that it is done in the most thorough and artistic manner.[29]

Mead's letter reached Mrs. Stanford at a time of great financial stress. Her husband's death, the railroad crisis and depression of 1893, and a contingent claim brought by the U.S. government against the Stanford estate for just over $15 million dollars—Leland Stanford's share, with interest, of construction loans made previously to the Central Pacific Railroad—had tied up her funds in a way that made it hard to know if the University itself would survive. Although resolved in Mrs. Stanford's favor by 1896, the immediate crisis and three more years

of financial difficulty may have caused her to line up solidly behind Mead as the less expensive artist and behind bronze as the less expensive medium. In any event, on a visit to Mead in Florence in 1899, Mrs. Stanford suggested some minor changes in his model before having it cast in bronze. Although she was never happy about the finished version, by December 1900 the life-size group was in place, not in the Museum as originally planned, but in the center of the University's inner quad on a stone pedestal (83).

82 *Larkin Mead's model for the Stanford sculpture was changed very slightly in the finished version.*

59

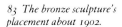

83 *The bronze sculpture's placement about 1902.*

THE MUSEUM'S OPENING YEARS,
1893–1900

Throughout the decade of the 1890s, the University and the Museum absorbed Mrs. Stanford's considerable energies. "There is so much work to do in the Museum," she wrote to a young friend shortly after her husband's death. "I dislike to be away from here. I feel as if this was home in the truest sense for here is all that [is] dearest that is left to me . . . of my loved ones."[30] The friend to whom she wrote was Timothy Hopkins, the adopted son of Mark Hopkins. Both Timothy and wife, the former May Crittenden, were special friends, whose wedding Jane Stanford had attended in New York in 1882 with her son. Because of her affection for the couple, Hopkins was one of the few people whose benefactions to the Museum were encouraged by Mrs. Stanford.[31]

Among the earliest of Hopkins' gifts were two hundred Korean objects bought from Henry G. Appenzeller, who had collected them while serving as a Methodist missionary in Korea (84).[32] Included were textiles, swords,

bowls, and an embroidered ten-panel screen or *chek kori* (85), which Appenzeller conveyed to San Francisco at the beginning of a furlough which brought him to the World's Columbian Exposition in Chicago in 1893, where Korean products were represented in the United States for the first time.

Although the fair contained several exhibits that later found their way to the Stanford Museum, one memorable piece was not among them: the two fountains spewing jets of wine and brandy that stood at the entrance to Stanford's Vina Vineyard exhibit.[33] The making of wine on his vast holdings in Tehama County was one of Stanford's many interests. Four thousand acres on the upper Sacramento River were given over to wine production managed by skilled winemakers whom Stanford had imported from France. Among the earlier plantings were Berger, Blanc Elben, Charbonneau, Malvoisie, and Zinfandel grapes. The remaining fifty-one thousand acres were used for fruit orchards, prize Holstein cows, and race horses, subjects that were depicted in panels hung in the art exhibit of the California pavilion. Four of these panels, executed in opaque watercolor on cotton canvas, remain in the Collection.

84 Henry G. Appenzeller, a Methodist missionary in Korea, with the costumes and screen he sold to the Stanford Museum in 1893. (SM 9519)

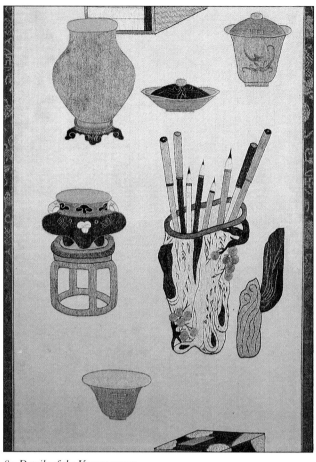

*85 Details of the Korean screen
seen in the background of the
photograph at left.* (SM 9685)

Another exhibitor from San Francisco was John Daggett, who displayed in the State building's historical exhibit a collection of Indian curios that was later purchased by Jane Stanford. Daggett had leased mining interests in the Siskiyou Mountains since the 1850s, and he had become friendly with the Indians from the area around the Klamath River and its tributaries who worked for him at the Doe and Daggett, the Black Bear, the Live Yankee, and other mines along the Upper Trinity River. Described in the fair's Official Report, Daggett's collection comprised

wearing apparel, ornaments, games, food products so arranged as to illustrate methods of procuring and preparing same, Indian baskets, stone and elk-horn utensils, fish nets, bows and arrows with fox-skin quiver, obsidian from which arrow points are made, money with elk-horn purse, pipes, comb, caps, baby baskets, etc.[34]

One of the seven original commissioners who planned California's contribution to the Chicago fair, Daggett resigned in 1893 when he was appointed superintendent of the U.S. Mint at San Francisco. He was living in the town of Black Bear in the Siskiyous in 1899, when Mrs. Stanford, who often visited those mountains, paid him for all the curios that had been on loan to the Museum since the closing of the fair, thereby securing permanently the fine baskets made by the Yurok, Karok, and Hupa Indians (86), as well as an eighteen-foot Yurok redwood canoe.[35]

Twenty-four watercolors of the California missions by Henry Chapman Ford, also on display in the historical exhibit at the California State building, were acquired by Jane Stanford from the fair (87). Ford, born in Lavonia, New York, had come to Santa Barbara for his

86 Baskets made by the Pomo and Hupa Indians seen in a   *photograph of the 1890s.*
(SM 13858)

health; from 1876 to 1882 he traveled up and down the state recording the then-ruinous buildings in watercolors and etchings.[36] (His etchings were on display in the fair's art exhibit, where Thomas Hill's painting *Driving the Last Spike* dominated the West Gallery.) Ford's studies of the missions were evidently carried out in the company of the photographer Carleton E. Watkins, whose photographs of the buildings date from the same years. The two upstate New Yorkers joined a party of artists, writers, and scientists who spent six weeks together at Yosemite during the summer of 1878 studying, sketching, and photographing the flora and fauna of the Valley.

Although Ford's carefully observed studies of the Spanish Colonial missions are thoughtful mementos of the nineteenth-century artist's interest in the land and in painting out-of-doors, they are also significant documents of the awakening American consciousness of the picturesque qualities of the West and of its rich historical heritage. Between 1884 and 1886, Hubert Howe Bancroft published his monumental *History of California;* and in 1883 and 1884, the novelist Helen Hunt Jackson wrote for the *Century Magazine* two popular stories that were to invite a romantic interest in the missions, "Father Junipero and His Work," and "The Present Condition of the Mission Indians."

That the Stanfords were among the first Californians to be attracted to the Spanish Mission style is seen in the patios and colonnades of the campus they first began to plan in 1886, and in the name they adopted from the estate they had bought—Rancho San Francisquito Palo Alto. Mrs. Stanford's personal interest in the Franciscan missions dated from the early eighties when she had contributed funds to her friend Fr. Angelo Casanova of the Monterey parish for the repair of the Mission San Carlos Borromeo in Carmel. In return, Fr. Casanova presented her in 1888 with an important group of mission music manuscripts—a large choirbook bound in rawhide containing thirty-six parchment pages, a sheath of closely written sheets and four separate parchment pages.[37] Together with a model of the Carmel mission built especially for the Stanford Museum, all of the material formed part of a display on the early history of California.

87 Henry Chapman Ford's watercolor, Mission San Carlos Borromeo, Carmel, *was exhibited at the Chicago Fair in 1893.*
(SM 63.94)

The Last Spike (39), symbolically tapped by Governor Stanford into the Last Tie joining the transcontinental railroad in 1869, was the inspiration of David Hewes (1822–1915), who had it cast in gold and engraved with the prayer "May God continue the unity of Our Country as this Railroad unites the two great oceans of the world." Hewes presented the Last Spike to the Stanford Museum in 1892 together with a substantial art collection. A San Francisco builder and financier, Hewes was born in Lynnfield, Massachusetts, and educated at Andover and Yale. He married as his second wife Jane Stanford's sister, Anna Maria Lathrop (1832–1892), in 1889, when she was a fifty-seven-year-old spinster and he a widower of recent date.[38] Years later, Hewes recalled that he met Anna Maria for the first time the evening he presented the Spike to Stanford for the upcoming grand occasion at Promontory, Utah. Hewes described the circumstances of its casting in a letter to Harry C. Peterson, curator of the Museum, who had asked for an account to accompany the exhibit:

The spike was cast (three or four times before we got a perfect one) by William T. Garrett Foundry and I remember each time we had to recast it. The mould was made the size and form of a regular RR spike.... A rough nugget about the size of the spike ... was jammed on the thin end of the spike by about 1/16th of thickness and the Governor broke off this nugget at my request to have rings made.... I threw ... in an extra twenty-dollar gold piece to increase the size of the nugget as I felt that souvenirs ... would be desired by many friends.... My first meeting with dear Anna was the evening I presented the Governor with the spike.[39]

One of the rings was for Anna Maria, one for Jane, and the biggest for Leland Stanford; the rest of the gold Hewes had made into miniature gold spikes and rings for other friends. Hewes also told Peterson that he had presented for use at Promontory the Last Tie, made of polished laurelwood to which he had attached a silver plate about six inches by eight inches inscribed with the names of the officers of the railroad. (The Tie was later placed in the offices of the Southern Pacific, where it was destroyed in the fire of 1906.)

But from Jane Stanford's viewpoint, Hewes's most important gifts to the Stanford Museum were Egyptian, material that first aroused his interest in 1876, when he chartered a private boat for travel up the Nile with his first wife, Mathilda French Gray, and her daughter and sister. Hewes returned to Cairo the next year, leaving the ladies in Mentone for three months (his wife was not well). Joined this time by his nephew, Granville S. Abbott, a Baptist minister, Hewes traveled by steamer for twenty days in February in the company of a superlative chronicler, the radical American theologian Dr. Philip Schaff, professor of Biblical Learning at Union Theological Seminary and president of the American Committee for Revision of the Authorized Version of the Bible.

"Our company consists," Schaff wrote in his erudite and entertaining account of the trip, "of forty-seven persons, English, Scotch, and Americans—clergymen, merchants, manufacturers, colonels, captains, two lords, and five ladies."[40] All got along pleasantly, he said, though they differed widely in taste and occupation. The dragoman was a Moslem from Luxor—"intelligent, obliging, and humorous"—who spoke English fluently, but could not read it. The ship's doctor was Greek, "more ornamental that useful"—he left his medicines behind and joined in all the excursions. Schaff's account, *Through Bible Lands* (1878), was one of hundreds of books on Egypt and the Holy Land that poured from the press at this time. Just as nineteenth-century classical scholars like Schliemann sought the historical Homer, Biblical scholars pursued the historical Jesus and the ancestors of Christ. Hewes's visit of 1877 can be followed in detail from Schaff's account. The trip, which lasted for three weeks in February, was by steamer chartered from the khedive by Thomas Cook and Sons. Passengers paid $235 for the twenty-day trip to the first cataract and back.

During his travels, Hewes made the acquaintance of a celebrated German Egyptologist, Heinrich Brugsch, whose scholarly interest lay in the Exodus and its pharaoh.[41] From 1870 to 1879, Brugsch, given the title bey by the khedive, directed the School of Egyptology in Cairo founded by the khedive in his efforts to modernize the country. Through the agency of Brugsch, Hewes was able to buy an encased mummy of a child as well as scarabs, vases, statuettes, and amulets from various tombs. All were recorded as being from Thebes of the Eighteenth and Nineteenth dynasties. Regrettably, the mummy was crushed beyond salvage in the earthquake of 1906, which brought down the Stanford Museum's entire Egyptian wing, and the smaller objects were scrambled with later acquisitions of Jane Stanford; it was never again possible to reconstitute the Hewes Collection in its entirety.

In Bulak, a suburb of Cairo on the right bank of the Nile, the party visited the museum that impressed Mrs. Stanford significantly on her later visit in 1901. Founded by the famous French archaeologist Mariette, the Bulak Museum held one of the richest collections in the world of Egyptian antiquities, some of which were for sale.

But as Schaff noted in 1877, the building was too small, and a larger one was being built on the other side of the Nile for the Cairo Museum.

After leaving Egypt, Hewes continued on his travels, just as Mrs. Stanford did years later, with visits to Jerusalem, the Dead Sea, Jordan, Galilee, and Damascus; and he later referred to the trip as "one of the most important and interesting" periods of his life. Earlier, Hewes had visited Athens and the Greek Islands. When he returned to San Francisco in 1878, he attempted to raise funds to buy Delphi for the American Institute. But Leland Stanford, the principal backer to whom Hewes turned, was too deeply immersed at that time in railroad business to investigate the project, so nothing came of it.

In Oakland, Hewes bought an Italianate villa on the shores of Lake Merritt in which he installed the collection he and his first wife had formed abroad and which later came to the Stanford Museum. Among the purchases acquired in Italy were seventeen sculptures in Carrara marble by contemporary Italians whose identities, with one exception, are not known. The exception was F. Mariotti, maker of the figure of *Astronomy* (88), which still remains in the Museum. From the catalogue Hewes had printed of his collection in 1888, we have the titles of the remaining sixteen, but for the most part these were smashed in the earthquake (89) and after repair, sold: *Moorish Dancing Girl, Flower Girl, Cupids Contending over a Heart, Infant Bacchus, Vanity* ("a little girl hanging cherries on her ears for ear-rings"), *Mischief* ("a little girl has seized a basket . . . and rushed out in the wind; she is standing with her feet firmly together, her dress blown back . . .") *The Waking Baby, The Boy with the Rabbit, The Boy with the Game, The Fortune Teller, Fidelity* ("a woman with a pet dog"), *A Child Gathering Flowers and Falling off the Rocks,* et cetera.

Hewes also brought back sixty-five terracotta statuettes reproducing antique sculptures like the Dancing Faun, the Medici Venus, and busts of the ancients, including Homer, Seneca, and Socrates, and of the moderns Petrarch, Dante, and Ariosto. (Not one remains

64

88 Mariotti's Astronomy *was the star of the Hewes collection before it was knocked off its pedestal in 1906 and broken into three pieces.*

89 Hewes's copies of Old Master paintings were unharmed by the earthquake.

in the Museum today.) Alabaster replicas also were acquired of the Baptistery and Tower of Pisa, the Three Graces, Michelangelo's Moses, and Julius Caesar. Like Mrs. Stanford, Hewes bought a bronze copy of the Farnese Bull and several mosaic tables, and he owned a copy of Raphael's *Madonna of the Chair*. Indeed, paintings in the Hewes Collection were largely copies of the Old Masters, copies which gave rise years later to the erroneous impression that the Stanford Museum contained no original paintings. Hewes's copies were after works by Fra Angelico, Raphael, Giorgione, Giulio Romano, Guido Reni, Murillo, Claude Lorraine, Domenichino, Correggio, Sassaferratto, Schedone, Canaletto, Rubens, Carlo Dolci, Raphael Mengs, and Salvator Rosa.[42]

After the death of his first wife in 1887, Hewes returned to San Francisco with his collection and became reacquainted with Mrs. Stanford's sister, whom he married in June 1889. A few days before the wedding, Hewes drew up a document transferring his paintings and sculptures, which he listed in full, to his bride-to-be.[43] In it he stated that it was his wish that the Anna Lathrop Hewes Collection should ultimately be placed in the Stanford Museum.

In 1889, now with Anna Maria as his bride, Hewes embarked on a second wedding trip to Europe and the Middle East, adding yet other replicas in bronze and oil to his collection of Old Master copies. Returning to Cairo in March 1890, he bought three "beautifully encased" mummies; at the same time, Mrs. Hewes bought material of a decidedly didactic character for the Stanford Museum with a thousand dollars given her for this purpose by Jane Stanford. Plaster casts of major monuments, as well as contemporary paintings of tomb cartouches, were requested and the material was provided by Emil Brugsch (1842–1930), a curator at the Bulak Museum who was to serve as Mrs. Stanford's buying agent in 1901. Brugsch had first come to Egypt with his older brother Heinrich in 1870 and had served as Mariette's assistant at the Bulak Museum and as curator under Maspero in Cairo. Hewes had not met him on his previous trip because Brugsch had spent 1876–77 in Philadelphia as commissioner for the Egyptian Government during the Centennial, or so Brugsch told Mrs. Stanford in a letter written after meeting her sister.

Seizing the opportunity to put himself forward, Brugsch said that it gave him "special pleasure to be able to render some service to the University created by Senator Mr. Leland Stanford in memory of a beloved son."[44] He wished he could do more, and he assured Mrs. Stanford that he had taken "all possible care" in carrying

90 Anna Maria Lathrop in a photograph taken by her nephew about 1881.

out the wishes of her sister and brother-in-law. He also told her that he had lived in San Francisco for seven years in the 1860s and would never forget his life there. He had many American friends, he said, and was also well acquainted with General Grant, whom he had accompanied on a four week trip up the Nile. (For his part, Grant, who visited Egypt in January, 1878, found Brugsch an indispensable guide: "What a blank our trip would be without Brugsch," the former president remarked to John Russell Young, the newspaper reporter who accompanied him, as the two came back from a ruin that their "fine young friend had made as luminous as a page in Herodotus."[45])

91 David Hewes in old age with the Museum's curator, Harry Peterson, and his wife (far right) and Mrs. Granville Abbott at Hewes's home in Orange County, 1914.

92 The Egyptian gallery around 1900 with a plaster cast of the Seated Cephren *from the Cairo Museum in the foreground.*

Brugsch provided Mrs. Stanford with many drawings, twenty-four plaster casts of the major monuments in the Bulak Museum, of which only the figure of the Seated Cephren survived the earthquake (92), and a seventeenth- or eighteenth-century Turkish Koran, three feet by two feet (93). Its seventy-six sheets were illuminated

93 Detail of a page from a Koran sold to Mrs. Stanford by Emil Brugsch in 1890. (SM 85.45)

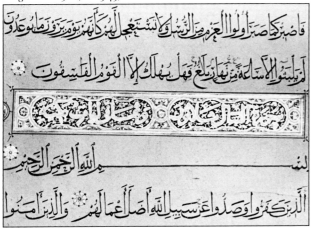

in gold and colors—leading Brugsch to doubt that Mrs. Stanford could find another like it in America.[46] In addition, Brugsch was an excellent photographer who prepared most of the plates for the *Catalogue Général* of the Bulak Museum. He sent directly to Mrs. Stanford in Washington some 120 photographs he had taken of important monuments in Upper Egypt, including the Tomb of the Royal Mummies, which he had first entered in 1881. Brugsch was quite accustomed to selling antiquities and plasters to Americans either from a shop on the premises of the Bulak Museum maintained for this purpose or as a middleman in other deals.

Satisfied with their own purchases, the Heweses returned to California, where in 1892 Mrs. Hewes died, bequeathing her husband's entire collection to the Stanford Museum as they had agreed to do at the time of their wedding. In 1903, Hewes printed a catalogue, *The Anna Lathrop Hewes Art Collection in the Stanford Museum,* and sent two dozen copies to Mrs. Stanford for her approval. He complained to Peterson that he never heard a word from her about them, nor did she credit him for the many things he had bought in Egypt, or for the Last Spike. "By whose oversight or fault," Hewes said, he did not know.[47]

Jane Stanford, Director

Among the acquisitions of 1893 that were most appreciated by Mrs. Stanford were several dozen Coptic textiles given her by Timothy Hopkins. They came to Hopkins in Cairo from Sir Flinders Petrie, who had excavated them in the Fayum district about sixty miles south of Cairo in 1889–90. In thanking Hopkins for the "mummy cloths," which date from the third to the mid-seventh century,[48] Jane Stanford wrote: "All the time I was looking at them I could not but exclaim how my dear boy would have reveled in the enjoyment of such a prize as you have bestowed and how he would have valued your sympathy and helpfulness." (109)[49]

With the opening of the Museum to the general public in 1893, Mrs. Stanford hired her first curator, John Kinlay Wright, who had just received his Stanford degree. Wright remained for two years, going on to the practice of law in New York City. Each year for the next four, curators arrived and departed, each recruited from the ranks of recent graduates: Percival J. Schlobach (1896), August Wollenschlager (1897), Arthur W. Thomas (1898), and Henry Clay Faber (1899). Finally, in Harry C. Peterson a person was found who could meet the Museum's demands in its earliest days, and Peterson remained from 1900 until 1917 (94). Loyal, hard-working, self-sacrificing, and underpaid, Peterson had been an unmatriculated student in the shops and engineering department with some experience gathering Western ornithological specimens for the British Museum before he joined the Stanford staff. Four galleries were partially filled when he took charge, and by the time of the earthquake twenty-three more had been completed. "During these years," he later wrote, "the entire responsibility of the Museum, its up-keep, the receipt and installation of the exhibits, the school talks and the entertainment of the many noted visitors of Mrs. Stanford, all fell upon my shoulders."[50] Nonetheless, if new paintings arrived when Mrs. Stanford was out of town, he was not permitted to install them. "I have to follow Mrs. Stanford's orders in all matters connected with the Museum," he wrote in 1902; "I have no discretion in the matter at all."[51]

After the earthquake, Peterson and five assistants worked from five in the morning until eight at night for six months, seven days a week, to salvage and reorganize the collection. Why did he do it? Well, as he wrote to the University's president in 1917, he thought his close connection with Mrs. Stanford had been the compelling force. "She was a wonderful woman," he wrote to Ray Lyman Wilbur in a desperate plea to keep the Museum open. And Peterson told how Mrs. Stanford had often broken down in tears and sobbed out her fear that the Collection—that of Leland Stanford Junior in particular—would one day be scattered "ruthlessly" by strange hands. "You have never had, as I have had, not once, but often, Mrs. Stanford put her face in her hands on your shoulder and break out crying."[52]

Until her death in 1905 at the age of seventy-seven, Mrs. Stanford continued to do all the buying for the Collection, spending time each year seeking out new materials, criss-crossing the United States in her private railroad car, traveling frequently to England, France, Italy, and Germany, and making two buying trips to Egypt and Japan between 1901 and 1904. She was often accompanied by Bertha Berner, who became her secretary after the death of Leland Stanford Junior and later wrote a memoir, *Mrs. Leland Stanford,* that touched on their travels together. One of these trips yielded an unusual *objet d'art*. In 1898, when Mrs. Stanford's funds were still enmeshed by legal difficulties, she attempted to raise money for the University by selling her jewels in London during Queen Victoria's Jubilee, an unsuccessful

94 Harry Peterson, the Museum's curator from 1900 to 1917.

68

project, but one that gave rise to a painting that the critic Alfred Frankenstein bemusedly described as "one of the most extraordinary still lifes in the history of American art" (95).[53] Before putting her diamonds, rubies, emeralds, sapphires, and pearls on the London market, she had a photograph taken of the jewelry her husband had given her over many years. (One of the sets had been bought from Tiffany's in Paris during the family's visit of 1881, when it had been described by the gossip columnist of the *American Register* as one of "the most magnificent sets of jewels ever got up in Paris for an American lady."[54]) As Bertha Berner tells it, the photograph taken by Taber Studio turned out so well that Mrs. Stanford decided to have a painting done that would represent the exact size and color of the stones. To do the work, she hired an eccentric painter from nearby San Jose, Astley David Montague Cooper (1856–1924).

Cooper's painting depicted the jewels on a canvas slightly larger than four feet by six feet, the execution of which was given an assist by generous gulps from a pocket flask. "Now you watch me put a little fire into that sapphire," he told Berner.[55] Unbeknownst to Mrs. Stanford, Cooper also painted a replica of the jewels on a redwood panel, which he hoped to sell by showing it in

the window of a gambling saloon in his home town. (It may actually have hung over the bar.) The police passed on the news to Mrs. Stanford who, chagrined, asked that the panel be removed. Despite the incident, her feelings about Cooper as a painter did not sour. She continued to admire his talent and, like the Roman matron in the story, she entrusted her other jewels to him as well, commissioning him to copy in oil that same year photographs of her husband and her son. (Cooper had previously executed a portrait of her sister Anna Maria in 1889.) Moreover, in addition to the four family-related portraits, Jane Stanford acquired a *Winter Landscape with Man and Dog* by Cooper as well as *Indians Hunting Buffalo* and *Indian on a White Horse*. (Born in Missouri, Cooper had begun painting Indian scenes before his twenty-first year.[56]) Mrs. Stanford probably bought Cooper's paintings of the Indians in 1900, the year she acquired from J. O. Coleman two famous paintings by Charles Christian Nahl that had been hanging in the Capitol building in Sacramento: *Crossing the Plains*, 1856 (96), and *Saturday Night at the Mines*, 1851 (97). With these acquisitions she returned again to scenes of the American West like Gideon Jacques Denny's *Indians on the Plain* that had first attracted her husband.

The Thomas Welton Stanford Collection

A parallel to Leland Stanford's collection of California landscapes was the group of Australian paintings acquired by his brother Thomas Welton Stanford (1832–1918) in Melbourne and sent to the Leland Stanford Junior Museum in shipments of 1897, 1905, and 1918. The sole collection of its kind in the United States, it recapitulated the history of colonial painting from the 1830s, when the painter John Glover came to Australia from London, to the decade of the 1860s, which saw the arrival of three important artists: the Swiss-born Louis Buvelot, the Austrian Eugen Von Guérard, and the Russian Nicholas Chevalier. Welton Stanford himself, the most eccentric of the six Stanford brothers, arrived in Australia from New York in 1860 and never returned to the States, though he sent back a fortune to Palo Alto in support of painting and parapsychology (98).

70

Successful as a merchant dealing in miners' supplies and later in Singer sewing machines,[57] Welton Stanford married in 1869, but was widowed the following year, a loss that undoubtedly contributed to his interest in the Victorian Association of Progressive Spiritualists, which

98 Thomas Welton Stanford, *about 1869, oil on canvas by Ebenezer Wake Cook.* (SM 14898)

99 George Earl, On the Yorkshire Moors, *1888, oil on canvas.* (SM 11809)

he founded with others in 1870.[58] The Association's monthly publication, *Harbinger of Light,* was published from Stanford's home, a mansion on Clarendon Street in East Melbourne (now the site of the Freemason's Hospital) with a picture gallery, a garden full of rare plants, and two acres of lofty aviaries one hundred feet high.

When the American spiritualist, Addie L. Ballou (1837–1916), came to Melbourne in 1886 to lecture under the auspices of the Association, she stayed on as Stanford's guest for three years. Reportedly gifted as a clairvoyant, Mrs. Ballou is said to have interrupted a lecture she was giving in Mankato, Minnesota, on the night of April 14, 1865, with the news of Lincoln's assassination—"A tragedy in Washington!"—though the town had no telegraph to connect it with the Capitol. Born in Ohio, Addie Ballou came to San Francisco in 1870, after having served as a nurse during the Civil War. In California she taught herself to paint, and by 1879 had established herself as an artist, maintaining a studio on lower Market Street for many years. A notary public in San Francisco just after the turn of the century, she played a role in the controversy surrounding the apports that Welton Stanford had received from the Great Beyond in seances held by the medium Charles Bailey and which Stanford wished to give to the University. Ancient coins, Assyrian tablets, and Egyptian scarabs from the hands of the dead had rained on Bailey while he was locked in a closet at Stanford House. Jane Stanford purportedly believed, but only according to Mrs. Ballou, that the collection was genuinely ancient and wished to have it exhibited at the University; but David Starr Jordan did not.[59]

Mrs. Ballou painted the only nude in Welton Stanford's collection, a work of 1874 entitled *Morning,* which represented a young woman "just awakening from sleep, poised tip-toe upon a globe, while the first light of morning steals through the sky." She also executed a portrait of Welton Stanford, as well as a study of a parrot from his aviary and flowers from his garden.

Stanford, who owned several horses and dogs, and kept muzzle-loading six-shooters, was a crack shot whose taste for the hunt was reflected in other pictures that he bought for himself and subsequently shipped to the Stanford Museum. *Gillie Holding Dogs and Watching the Effect of a Shot, Stag and Hind, Otters and Salmon,* and numerous other works by James Giles, George Earl (99), and other Scots and English painters in the tradition of Landseer were among the 105 paintings Welton Stanford owned in 1892 when his collection was catalogued by Sidney Dickinson,[60] an American art critic and popular

100 After Frans Snyders, Dog with Head of a Cow, *oil on canvas.* (SM 11863)

lecturer who had come to Sydney from San Francisco reportedly as the Australian correspondent of the *New York Herald.*[61] Dickinson was strong on subject matter, but not as keen on technique. Two ferocious scenes of snarling beasts of prey in the Stanford Collection, attributed by him to Frans Snyders, are now believed to be later copies; *Dog with Head of a Cow* (100) is perhaps by the Italian Felice Boselli (1650–1732). A third painting with Baroque origins was *Dead Game* by Jan Weenix (101), recorded by Dickinson as having been

101 Attributed to Jan Weenix, Dead Game, *oil on canvas.* (SM 11880)

71

102 Louis Buvelot, Landscape near Fernshaw, *1875, oil on canvas.* (Present whereabouts unknown)

brought out of Paris during the Revolution by Madame Du Barry and to Australia by a Dr. Waite, from whom Stanford bought the huge canvas.

Still other paintings were selected by Welton Stanford at the Melbourne Exhibition of 1888, "with much care and thought," he wrote, "each because of its intrinsic merit, uninfluenced by the name of the painter."[62] Dickinson pronounced Stanford's collection of Australian landscapes far and away the best such collection in Melbourne. The group included nine paintings by the Impressionist Buvelot (102), as well as canvases by John Glover, K. U. Bennett, Nicholas Chevalier, Ebenezer Wake Cook (98), Eugen Von Guérard, H. J. Johnstone, J. McDonald, John White, and Isaac Whitehead. To these were joined 119 oils and watercolors by the Devonshire-born James Waltham Curtis, a painter of the Australian outback whom Stanford frequently accompanied on horseback trips to the most beautiful areas of Queensland.

In 1897, Welton Stanford dispatched sixty Curtis watercolors to the Museum in Palo Alto, and this group was followed by another in 1905 of eighty-three paintings by Australian, European, and American painters. Finally, in 1918, a third shipment arrived, the paintings bequeathed to the Museum with Stanford's estate. Among the latter was Thomas Hill's *Mount Shasta,* evidently a gift from Leland and Jane Stanford's original collection and now returned once more to California (103). Welton

103 Thomas Hill, Mount Shasta,
c. 1876, oil on canvas. (SM 76.24)

Stanford's beneficence was prompted, he wrote in 1910, by the prospect of pleasure to be derived by Stanford students and visitors from viewing the paintings coupled with a desire to avoid probate duty. The next year, he sent a gift of $100,000 to the University for the restoration of the Museum, which had been badly damaged in the earthquake. All the paintings Stanford had given previously had survived the tremor, and he wanted to ensure that there was a gallery for their display. (After his death in 1918 the money was used for the construction of the Thomas Welton Stanford Art Gallery near the center of the campus.) On this occasion he frankly admitted that he had recently reduced his holdings in order "to escape the excessive gradations of a class land tax of a most villainous character." He explained: "Directly the laborites gained a majority in the Common Wealth Parliament, they began a crusade against the owners of land in

town and country, and as quickly as possible passed a class land tax."[63] With the proceeds from the same divestiture, Stanford gave the University $50,000 for research into psychic phenomena.

Only one of the nearly 150 Australian landscapes formerly in the Museum's collection remains at Stanford. The others were either lost, sold, or given away, primarily during the period from 1917 to 1952, when the building lay in ruins and local collectors and dealers could wander through it at will. Tens of thousands of objects were lost over these years through neglect, pilferage, or ill-advised sale. The single remaining landscape, *Horseman Fording a Stream* by J. W. Curtis, was returned to the Museum in 1962, with numerous other long-lost objects, from the estate of the Museum's director from 1917 to 1945, Pedro Lemos.

ON A TRIP to Europe in 1899, after her financial problems were solved, Mrs. Stanford opened negotiations with a Venetian mosaic and glassmaking firm, Salviati and Company, for a major commission: the mosaic decoration not only of the Museum's exterior but also of the Stanford Church being built at the center of the University campus as a memorial to Leland Stanford. Originally conceived in the 1880s by the architect Charles Coolidge, one of Richardson's successors, and subsequently enlarged by Clinton Day of San Francisco, the Church was designed in a Byzantine-Romanesque style.[64] In Mrs. Stanford's mind, mosaic decoration was called for: years before, with her husband and son, she had visited St. Mark's in Venice and Byzantine churches in Constantinople, where she had seen the iridescent effect of the mosaic picture. The Salviati shop, too, was familiar to her from the 1883 trip. Moreover, Antonio Salviati (1816–1890), an innovator in the making of Venetian glass and mosaic, had restored the centuries-old mosaics in St. Mark's. By 1899, the Salviati firm with its many artists, designers, mosaicists, and glassmakers had been taken over by Mauricio Camerino, who spoke English fluently, and it was to him that Mrs. Stanford turned when the Church's construction was begun. In Camerino's case, too, there was a sentimental recall: at the time of Leland Stanford Junior's death, Camerino had rushed to Florence to help the family by serving as an interpreter in dealing with the Italian authorities.

The Stanford Memorial Church was to be extensively embellished on both the exterior and the interior; its iconographic program was devised by Jane Stanford in conjunction with Camerino.[65] In Paris and Venice they looked at mosaics together and studied photographs of churches that Mrs. Stanford had been collecting. For the original designs, Camerino turned to his chief artist, Antonio Paoletti (1834–1912), a genre painter. The massive, exterior mosaic, *Christ Welcoming the Righteous into the Kingdom of God* (Matthew 25:34), was Paoletti's conception. And virtually all the interior walls are covered with mosaics designed originally in watercolor by him—a pastiche of figures based largely on sources in Raphael, Michelangelo, Guido Reni, and the Pre-Raphaelites. For the most part, they represent scenes from the Old Testament. The mosaic panel behind the altar, however, is a copy of Cosimo Roselli's *Last Supper* from the Sistine Chapel. By 1902, the Salviati mosaic

workshop had suspended all its other work in order to carry out the Stanford project. According to Camerino, Mrs. Stanford had given her country "the finest and biggest piece of monumental mosaic work up to date"[66] and he could only wish that there were a "few ladies of her liberality in Italy."[67] (104, 105)

It is of interest to note that the Church's stained-glass windows were commissioned from the American firm of Frederick Stymetz Lamb, Mrs. Stanford's choice after visiting the Lamb, the Tiffany, and the Gorham studios. Although she considered Lamb the most dedicated artist of the trio, very likely her choice had to do with the firm's specialization in ecclesiastical art; *Religion Enthroned,* a window that won two gold medals when it was exhibited at the Paris Exposition in 1900, was generally regarded as Lamb's finest work. At Stanford, nineteen large windows in the transept depict scenes from the life of Christ; others in the clerestory portray figures from both the Old and New Testaments, together with saints and evangelists. (At Mrs. Stanford's request, figures of women are prominent.) The Lamb windows reproduce paintings by Carlotti, Ernst Deger, Anton Dietrich, Gustave Doré, Axel Ender, Edward A. Fellowes-Prynne, William Holman Hunt, John Heinrich Hofmann, Antonio Paoletti, Sybil C. Parker, Bernard Plockhorst, and Frederick James Shields. Murillo's *Miracle of the Loaves and Fishes* is also included in recollection of Leland Stanford Junior's admiration for the Spanish Baroque painter.[68]

At the Museum, too, there was a connection between the decorations and the dead boy. Herbert Nash recounted that at Pompeii in 1881 Mrs. Stanford, placing a fragment of mosaic in young Leland's hands, had said: "Let this be the nucleus of your museum."[69] For its façade eight rectangular mosaic panels were installed in the following order: *Rome, Painting, Architecture, Egypt, Cyprus, Sculpture, Archaeology,* and *Progress and Civilization,* an iconographic program that makes an interesting comparison with Elihu Vedder's mural *Rome* or *The Art Idea,* executed in Italy in 1894 for the Walker Art Building at Bowdoin College. Additional panels proposed by Camerino in November 1904 for two wings being added at that time were not carried out, probably because of Mrs. Stanford's death three months later. This project consisted, Camerino wrote, "in showing all the different styles used up to date from the primitif to the New Art now in use. It will be extremely instructive to students who could call there and see at once which is the Roman, Celtic, Greek, Byzantine, Egyptian, Middle Age style, etc. It is a splendid project, quite fit for a Museum and I

74

104 *The Venetian workshop of*
Silvio Salviati (standing) *about*
1904 with the mosaic portrait of
Jane Stanford and cartoons for the
mosaics in the Stanford Church.

105 *In the Stanford Church,*
Salviati mosaics after designs
by Antonio Paoletti alternate
with stained glass windows by
Frederick Stymetz Lamb.
The large window to the left of
The Expulsion *mosaic is after*
a painting by the German
artist John Heinrich Hofmann,
The Home in Nazareth.

106 Antonio Paoletti, History, *c. 1901, watercolor design for a mosaic overdoor at the entrance to the Stanford Museum.* (SA)

76

obtained the permit to copy the tablets from our collection in the Correr Museum of Venice."[70]

Mrs. Stanford's comments on Camerino's earlier proposals were forthright and decisive, and it is evident that she knew exactly what she wanted from his shop. His submissions for three panels to be placed over the Museum's entrance doors, for example, met with the following reply:

Two I approve of, namely, History (106) and Ancient Art. The one of Modern Art I do not fancy. I think the two I have approved of, one should go to the left and one to the right as they would be facing each other, and for the middle panel I wish you to have a new design made showing a front view. . . . The Modern Art picture I do not like at all as the figure of the woman is not pleasing. It would suit as a decoration for a botanical building, but not for an Art Museum, containing a miscellaneous collection.[71]

Not surprisingly, moreover, she shared the Victorian dislike for empty space. This *horror vacui,* obvious in the finished results, turns up in her letters again and again:

I notice blank spaces over the other two outside doors in front of the building. Why could not these two blank spaces be cast in moulds with Egyptian and Greek figures—something pertaining to Antiquity.

I think the bronze doors might be patterned somewhat differently. They are severely plain with only the three squares in each door. Could not figures of griffins or something in antique style [be added] that would not cost any more than these which look somewhat like prison doors.[72]

And speaking of the Church, she wrote to Camerino:

You will see each side of the Transept has five double stained-glass windows, each window representing a single figure. . . . Following

these windows are large spaces of blank stone wall quite plain, and I have concluded to place mosaics to correspond with the colored glass windows in order to decorate this plain wall.[73]

Camerino, whose company was paid a total of $97,000 for the mosaic work at Stanford, did his best to carry out Mrs. Stanford's wishes. He not only came to California twice to inspect the results, but also presented the Museum with 200 Salviati reproductions of antique Venetian glass originals. And to further the interests of artists and craftsmen in Venice, he saw to it that woodcarving from the Mainella Company was displayed in the Stanford Museum together with old Venetian mirrors and Salviati glass chandeliers. A case in the Venetian room contained a display showing how his mosaics were made. Finally, at the Louisiana Purchase Exposition in St. Louis in 1904, he exhibited the five mosaic portraits his firm had executed after photographs of the three Stanfords and Mr. and Mrs. Charles Lathrop, Jane's brother and sister-in-law. Mrs. Stanford stopped to see them there as she made her way home from New York on her last transcontinental railroad journey (107).

107 Salviati's mosaic portrait of Jane Stanford was based on a photograph. (SM 11462)

COLLECTING, 1900–1905

A T THE SAME TIME that Mrs. Stanford opened negotiations with the Salviati firm, she also resumed the
habit of extravagant buying that had preceded her
husband's death, acquiring copies of the Old Masters, for
example, that she had resolved to have for the Museum
from the beginning. Already in 1889 she had received
the personal permission of the king of Saxony to negotiate
with a German artist, Karl Bertling, to execute a copy of
Raphael's *Sistine Madonna* in Dresden. But a year later
the commission went instead to Ludwig Sturm, who
copied the painting for her twice. Then, in 1891, a notice
appeared in the *Art Amateur* to the effect that the kings
of Italy and Belgium and the czar of Russia had granted
the Stanfords permission to have copies made of all the
historical pictures in their respective galleries, stipulating
only that the court painter be employed. The exact size
of the originals and the frames were also to be duplicated;
and the collection was to embrace modern masters as
well. Nine years passed before anything further came of
this plan to enrich the studies of Stanford art students in
the days before the color slide. Old museum records
indicate that during 1900 and 1901 a number of collections in Florence—the Uffizi Museum, the Pitti Palace,
and the Corsini, Feroni, and Demidoff galleries
—were the source of copies of Italian paintings: two
after Andrea del Sarto, one after Fra Bartolommeo, three
after Raphael, four after Titian, one after Correggio, two
after Carlo Dolci, one after Carlo Maratta, three after
Guido Reni, and one after Salvator Rosa. Copies of
paintings by Murillo and Greuze were also included.

By 1903, when the Museum's first catalogue was
published, the Old Master copies filled a small room on
the second floor. Elsewhere, the galleries were filled with
a variety of collections ranging from Egyptian, Greek,
and Roman to Chinese, Japanese, and Korean, intermingled, on the ground floor, with American Indian holdings
and, on the upper, with several dozen nineteenth-century
Italian sculptures and five hundred European and American paintings, largely by contemporary artists. Still other
paintings and sculptures from the Stanfords' Nob Hill
house were to be added with the bulk of Mrs. Stanford's
estate.[74]

A gallery on the upper floor, now used for the
Museum's program of changing exhibitions, was the
setting in Mrs. Stanford's day for the collection of family
memorabilia, which provoked ridicule from the begin-

ning. Here were displayed portraits of the Stanford and
Lathrop families, together with personal mementos of
Leland Stanford's life as president of the Central Pacific
Railroad, governor of California, and U.S. senator;
souvenirs of the couple's European travels were added,
as were Mrs. Stanford's Worth gowns, her lace collection,
the Muybridge photographs of the Horse in Motion,
letters from members of the Grant family and other
notables, and the like. Popularizing historians since her
time have mocked Jane Stanford for her sense of what
was appropriate for museum display.[75] She herself felt
a certain self-consciousness about the exhibits in the Memorial Room, asking Peterson not once but often to
indulge her. "When I'm gone," she told him, "go over it
and re-arrange it as may seem best to you." Peterson in
turn observed that Mrs. Stanford was well aware of her
mistakes but that she felt she ought to have the pleasure
of putting what she pleased in the Museum and arranging
it as she saw fit. "She said," he wrote to President Wilbur,
"that since she paid the bills we ought to indulge her to
that extent." Peterson added that he didn't want Wilbur
to have any mistaken ideas about what Mrs. Stanford
really thought of her memorial collections.[76]

Mrs. Stanford was also in the habit, Bertha Berner
explained, of using the Museum's storage area as a
warehouse for household goods she meant to sort at a
later date, but, like many a housewife, never did. Old
trunks containing china and glassware, linens, bric-a-
brac of all sorts, case upon case of eyeglasses, manicure
sets, leather goods, and much else stood for years in the
Museum's basement. During the interregnum from 1917
to 1945, much of the material that Mrs. Stanford meant
to discard was spread out for students and others to see.
Although few written records of the Museum's activities
were kept during those years, an occasional old grad
turns up who can still remember the Dickensian gloom
of the building when surveillance was at a minimum and
the curator slept in a bed by the front door. Into this
madcap setting, a student introduced as a joke an object
that has never been forgotten by those who toured the
premises in those forlorn years. This was a model in
porcelain of bacon and eggs on a plate with a label
attached to it that read: Little Leland's Last Breakfast. A
token of twentieth-century reaction against Victorian
sentimentalism, the hoax remained on view for the best
part of twenty years, an additional reminder, if one were
needed, of the scorn of the University community for the
Leland Stanford Junior Museum. In 1977, long after it
had been removed, the author of a history of American
museums commented straight-faced that out in Palo

Alto The Breakfast was thought to be reminiscent of Leonardo's *Last Supper*.[77]

Near the Memorial Room at the turn of the century was a gallery given over to the history of the University, material which has since become the basis of its archives. This contained the architectural plans and projects of the firm of Shepley, Rutan, and Coolidge, photographs of the construction of campus buildings, an exhibit based on the preparation of the mosaics for both the Museum and the Stanford Memorial Church, and other documents and records of the University's beginnings. The upper floor of one of the wings built in 1900 contained natural history exhibits—minerals, birds' eggs, and mounted mammals (108), which eventually included fur seals from the Pribilof Islands given by David Starr Jordan, mementos of an incident that nearly caused a war between Great Britain and the United States.

Nevertheless, the make-up of the Collection was episodic, as Peterson recognized. "No attempt was made to complete gaps either chronologically or historically," he explained to President Wilbur.[78] The Collection was made up, in the majority of cases, of isolated specimens. Mrs. Stanford's interest in American Indian artifacts, for example, had waned as she turned her attention increasingly to the Middle and Far East. In 1903, she turned down a chance to buy the Huckle Collection of fifty-six Navajo blankets offered her for about $15,000 and called to her attention by Dr. George Dorsey, director of the Field-Columbian Museum in Chicago, who could not afford to buy it for his own institution. Dorsey wrote to Peterson that "knowing Mrs. Stanford's taste in such matters and her desire to possess for her museum only the greatest and the best," it had occurred to him that she might like to buy the Collection, which included some "absolutely unique" blankets.[79]

108 Preparators working on natural history exhibits for the Museum, about 1900.

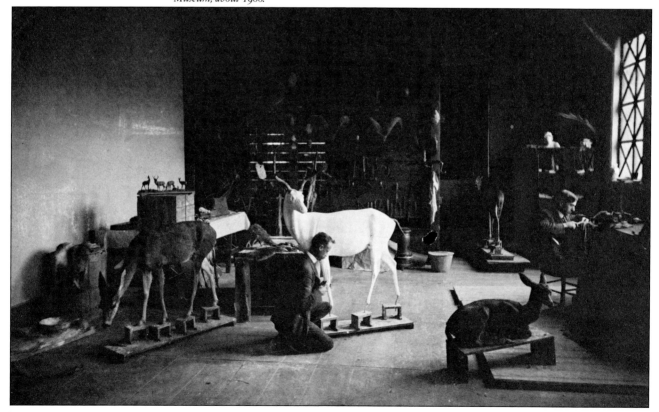

78

The year before, Dorsey had warned that Stanford's "glorious opportunity for building up a fine Pacific Coast museum" was being lost. "The University of California is forging ahead at a very rapid rate, so rapidly indeed, that it will only be a short time when it will be impossible for you to overtake them, no matter what amount of money you may have at your disposal, for conditions are changing very rapidly on the Pacific Coast."[80]

Dorsey was referring to Mrs. Phoebe Hearst's founding of a museum and a department of anthropology in 1901, and his words must have pained Mrs. Stanford. Rumor had it that the two women were fierce competitors on behalf of their respective institutions. A generous patron of the University of California, Phoebe Hearst was the widow of George Hearst, who had struck it rich decades earlier with a claim to part of the famous Comstock Lode. Her interests as a collector overlapped those of her friend at Stanford in several key areas, namely, the high cultures of the Mediterranean and the tribal societies of the New World. Since 1896, Mrs. Hearst had been supporting archaeological expeditions in Egypt, Greece, and Italy, in addition to funding excavations and research in Peru, California, the Southwest and the North American Indian Mounds. On a trip to Cairo in 1898, she had made the acquaintance of George Reisner, then director of Egyptian excavations for the American Exploration Society. She told Reisner of her plans to coordinate a few large subscribers for a strictly California enterprise, and the following year drew up a five-year contract with him for excavations "to be conducted in the name of such societies or Universities as shall be designated by Mrs. P. A. Hearst."[81] In view of Mrs. Stanford's special interest in Egyptian art, the proposition put to Reisner by Mrs. Hearst strikes a preëmptive note. But no documentation of rivalry surfaces in the polite notes exchanged by the two ladies during the 1890s, a decade which saw their return to San Francisco from Washington as widows in close succession. (George Hearst served as the Democratic senator to the U. S. Congress while Stanford was the Republican senator. Hearst died in 1890, three years before Stanford.)

Further, although the archaeological collections they amassed were similar in kind, their methods of procurement differed, and in the long run Mrs. Hearst had the advantage. Instead of buying previously formed collections on her own cognizance as Mrs. Stanford did, Mrs. Hearst worked closely with a number of scholars to fund excavations for objects that served the purposes of their research. Reisner was one; another was the eminent classicist Alfred Emerson with whom Mrs. Hearst made personal arrangements in 1899 for the purchase of Greco-Roman antiquities in Europe. To obtain additional collections for the University of California, she supported the work of the early generation of American anthropologists, Max Uhle in Peru, for example, and Philip Mills Jones in California. In 1906 the chairman of the university's distinguished department of anthropology, Frederic Ward Putnam, former head of Harvard's Peabody Museum, could write that as a result of Mrs. Hearst's support "the Department has been able, within the few years of its existence, to take rank among the foremost museums and institutions of anthropological research in the country."[82]

Mrs. Stanford was evidently aware that without the expertise of scholars in the field, the Stanford Museum could neither keep pace with Berkeley nor properly serve its own university, and in 1904, she wrote to Cesnola asking that he recommend a good museum man, but he could think of no one. So intent had she been on the material formation of the collection her son had projected that Mrs. Stanford had ignored the important matter of its scholarly presentation for too long. Of course, by the same token, it is not unlikely that for psychological reasons, Mrs. Stanford resisted the hiring of a qualified director since in her mind that person would serve as a surrogate for Leland Stanford Junior. In addition, the museum profession, in its infancy at this time, was faced with huge quantities of material gathered primarily during the second half of the nineteenth century and it was not easy to find curators who were equipped to make qualitative judgments about the leavings of the rich. Mrs. Stanford was apparently reluctant to spare Peterson for additional training on the East Coast, which he very much wanted to undertake. As a result, the good-natured Peterson did the best he could by consulting museum men like George Dorsey, who visited the Stanford Museum at least twice, Charles Loring, director of the Boston Museum of Fine Arts, and Cesnola at the Metropolitan. All three sent him samples of file cards and record books used in their respective museums, and Dorsey provided Peterson with general rules for classifying ethnological material. Putting practical information of this sort to use was the best Peterson could do by way of establishing professional standards for the Stanford Museum.

79

Timothy Hopkins and the Egypt Exploration Fund

Far more difficult for Peterson was the cataloguing of the large collection of ancient Egyptian material that had been accruing since 1893 with the gifts of David Hewes and Timothy Hopkins (109). More was to come, making the Museum's collections of Egyptian art substantial and valuable even today, despite the losses suffered in 1906 and during the long period of neglect that followed. For one thing, in addition to purchasing Egyptica directly, Hopkins also became a member in 1900 of the Egypt Exploration Society, a membership that stimulated periodic gifts to the Museum over the next eleven years.[83] (Members did not themselves receive objects, but those who gave generously to the Society could influence divisions to particular institutions.) First to arrive with the sponsorship of the Fund were bracelets, amulets, strings of beads, and pieces of stone vases excavated at Abydos in 1899–1900 and dating from prehistoric time to the Twelfth Dynasty. The Society's 1903–4 season produced, among other items, Eleventh Dynasty wooden boatmen and Eighteenth Dynasty pottery fragments from Naville's excavations at Deir el-Bahari, as well as fifty terracottas of the Roman period from Petrie's excavations at Ehnasya; and terracottas, seals, and glass, wooden, iron, and copper objects from Grenfell and Hunt's excavations at Oxyrhynchus.

In 1907, Hopkins's share in the Society's findings netted twenty objects from Deir el-Bahari, including limestone fragments from the Eleventh Dynasty temple of King Mentuhotep and eleven other artifacts found at Oxyrhynchus and dating from the third century. The year 1909 brought Eighteenth Dynasty ushabtis, faience, and seals from El Mahasna and Abydos. And finally, in 1911, the season's digging at Abydos yielded predynastic pottery, together with alabasters and limestone fragments of the Eighteenth Dynasty.

109 Coptic textile given to the Museum by Timothy Hopkins in 1893. (SM 14720)

Jane Stanford in Egypt

On a leisurely trip to Europe and the Middle East during 1900 and 1901, Mrs. Stanford finally met Emil Brugsch, the curator of the Cairo Museum who had dealt with her sister years before. Through Brugsch, she acquired two additional collections for Stanford. Before opening negotiations with him, however, she took a six-week cruise up the Nile in a dahabeah, the "Olga," with a crew of sixteen that she had hired from Thomas Cook.[84] Sailing from Cairo on January 29, 1901, she traveled with her secretary (and memorialist) Bertha Berner, bringing as guests the University's professor of Latin and Archaeology, Walter Miller, and his wife and daughter. At Luxor, the party was joined by an American Baptist minister, Chauncey Murch, who had been in Egypt since 1883 working for the United Presbyterian Board of Foreign Missions.

Murch was a collector with a special interest in scarabs who had made himself useful to many American and English visitors over the years, among them Charles Wilbour, whose valuable antiquities formed the beginnings of the superlative Egyptian collection at the Brooklyn Museum, and Ernest Budge, keeper of the Egyptian and Assyrian antiquities at the British Museum; Gaston Maspero, too, director of the Service des Antiquités, knew Murch well. Wilbour described him as a "fat parson . . . who preaches in Arabic and shows a fine collection of anteekah which he will sell from, as a favor to a friend."[85] Budge considered Murch both a sound businessman and a good friend of the British Museum, where three of Murch's scarab collections were placed. (When Murch died, his collection was divided between London and New York, the Metropolitan Museum receiving more than three thousand objects.)

Murch assisted Jane Stanford in selecting objects for the Museum, as well as acting as her guide to all the sights near Luxor. At Kena, the ladies sang hymns with him, and Mrs. Stanford invited Murch and his wife and son to the Nile boat for dinners specially prepared by the cook. Berner remarked that the Murches, having lived so long on the simple fare of the country, "frankly enjoyed the good dishes, especially plum pudding from Buzzard's in London, with a brandy sauce."[86]

After the party left Egypt, Murch wrote a long and effusive letter to Mrs. Stanford, telling her how precious the memory of her visit was to him and his wife. Before meeting her, he confessed, he doubted that a woman with such a colossal fortune would care to be approached by such as lived at Luxor. "How different we found it!" Among other things, he wanted to know if she had been

110 Jane Stanford (standing at center) *in Egypt in 1904.*

able to find the books on Egyptology that she had seen in his library and sought to buy for the University. At the time, he had already arranged to place them in the British Museum. But thinking about it later, he wanted her to know that if she had not yet been able to find them elsewhere, he was confident he could change the arrangements he had made. "The British Museum will be very glad . . . to grant the books in recognition of certain obligations . . . for assistance I have given them at various times in the acquisition of purchases they have made in Egypt."[87]

From Murch's library may have come the twenty-one volumes of the magnificent folio *Description de l'Egypte* that Mrs. Stanford presented to the University Museum upon her return from the trip. Commissioned by Napoleon and printed by the Imprimerie Royale in 1809, the *Description* was executed by dozens of scholars, scientists,

historians, and artists whose work formed an incomparable account of both ancient and modern Egypt. Its numerous engravings recorded with painstaking care details of both the natural and the man-made world—the living flora and fauna and the awesome ruined monuments—of the country that had so enthralled her son. She also gave the Museum a copy of Petrie's *Ten Years in Egypt* that had been presented to her in Cairo by the author.

Returning to Cairo in March after a trip that had taken her as far as Philae, Mrs. Stanford got in touch with Emil Brugsch. Through Brugsch, a middleman more than a dealer, she acquired two collections that Brugsch catalogued for her. The first came from a well-known dealer with a shop near Shepheard's Hotel, N. D. Kyticas, who is known to have sold to the Metropolitan and to the Boston Museum of Fine Arts and to have

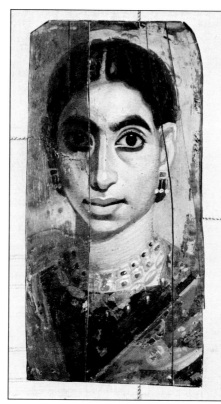

111 (left) Portrait of a Man, *tempera on wood, from the Fayum region, probably Er-Roubayat, 275–325 A.D.,* bought by Jane Stanford in 1901. (SM 22226)

112 Portrait of a Woman, *from the Fayum, encaustic on cypress wood, is one of the Egyptian objects sold by Kyticas in 1901.* (SM 22225)

been visited regularly by such collectors as Theodore Davis and J. Pierpont Morgan. From Kyticas, Mrs. Stanford acquired thirty-five objects, primarily of the Greco-Roman period, in which the dealer specialized.[88] Included were bronzes, cartonnage, gold jewelry, scarabs, and a male and female portrait from the Fayum district (111, 112). In all, the collection was "worthy," Maspero wrote in an accompanying document, "to be exhibited in any Museum of Europe or America."[89]

The second collection belonged to Brugsch's wife, who had assembled 273 objects over many years in Egypt. Evidently, Jane Stanford saw the collection in Cairo, but did not offer to buy it until she got to Kissingen in June, when she wrote to Brugsch mentioning five thousand dollars for it.[90] Brugsch replied, "If you would offer today three times the amount with the demand to make up a similar collection inside three or four years, I could not do so, objects are getting more and more rare and dearer every year."[91] Indeed, it was for this reason, Brugsch explained, that his wife no longer collected: "She does not want to keep on buying, prices have gone up so high, and herself therefore having lost all pleasure." A mixed

collection of minor arts, mostly funerary in nature and dating from predynastic to late, Mrs. Brugsch's holdings were typical of the pottery and stone objects that could be found in the debris of ancient Egyptian cities and cemeteries until late in the nineteenth century.

A fragment of a bronze offering table (113) was outstanding among the ushabti, amulets, alabasters, scarabs, and other bronzes of the collection. The scene was a king leading a procession of Hapi figures, and the fragment represented Hapi, God of the Nile, crowned with a clump of papyrus, symbol of Lower Egypt. The Stanford section is one of several from the same table found in Cairo, New York, Baltimore, Paris, and Hanover.[92]

In Egypt that year, Jane Stanford also met Petrie's countryman H. W. Seton-Karr, an introduction that produced many gifts from the British explorer. The first portion, which arrived in Palo Alto in July 1901, contained stone implements from the prehistoric flint mines at Wadi-el-Sheikh that were first discovered by Seton-Karr with the help of H. E. Johnson and the Arabs in 1896.[93] All stages of the manufacture of stone knives until

*113 Hapi, God of the Nile,
fragment of a bronze offering table
from Memphis, Late Dynastic
c. 700 B.C. (SM 21460)*

the McAdams collection of American mound relics, a collection of nearly 1,500 chipped-stone tools and artifacts representing the entire spectrum of Midwestern prehistory, from the Paleo-Indian to the Mississippian. Somewhat later, a collection totaling 784 flint tools from prehistoric Denmark was added. The knives in this collection are among the finest flint implements made anywhere in the world. Many are shaped like laurel leaves; others have been carefully fashioned to imitate metal prototypes, complete with seams and rivets, all in stone (115).

Stone implements continued to arrive at the Museum after Mrs. Stanford's death in 1905. When Seton-Karr came to see the display that Peterson had arranged, he arrived so soon after the earthquake that the material was buried in the rubble of modern times. Peterson was able, nonetheless, to recover practically every piece, although, as he wrote to Seton-Karr in July 1908, "they were all mixed in hopeless confusion" and had gotten so soaked during several days of rain that the labels pasted on them had in some cases come loose.[97] Peterson reported, too, that the Egyptian department had suffered more than any other; and, since he hoped to build it up again, he welcomed the donation of additional specimens. "We no longer have Mrs. Stanford with us," he wrote, "to open her purse strings and buy what is needed." A month later a case containing Indian paleolithic implements and various types of Egyptian chipped flint implements, principally from the Fayum district, was sent by Seton-Karr, together with two monographs to assist the curator in writing label copy. In return, Seton-Karr had one small request: "I should be glad if you would make

83

*114 Group of prehistoric Egyptian
knives found at Wadi-el-Sheikh by
H.W. Seton-Karr. (SM)*

the time of the Middle Kingdom were here represented (114).[94] A second group was dispatched to Stanford in 1903 by the Smithsonian Institution at Seton-Karr's request.[95] This comprised paleolithic implements collected in the lateritic deposits at Poondi, near Madras.

At the receiving end, Mrs. Stanford was especially pleased. "She is greatly interested in this department," wrote Peterson in a letter of thanks to Seton-Karr.[96] Prehistoric stone implements had been acquired for the Museum as early as 1885, when Mrs. Stanford bought

115 *Danish stone tools formed part of the large collection of* *prehistoric artifacts gathered by Jane Stanford for the Museum.* (SM)

a distinction in labelling or describing between those which have been found by the donor or explorer (namely myself) and gifts which have merely been purchased by the giver in a shop."[98]

The origins of the acquisitions gained by Mrs. Stanford during the eight weeks of her return trip to Egypt in 1904, however, have always presented something of a mystery; all the more so, since the range in quality of

116 *This limestone carving of the* Seated Cheops *was sold to Mrs. Stanford as an Old Kingdom sculpture.* (SM 66.373)

these ancient objects, dating from Old Kingdom to *circa* 1904, is so great. One certainty, however, is that Mohammed Ali el Gabri sold her twenty-seven pieces at Shepheard's Hotel on January 9, 1904, when he signed a paper attesting to their authenticity. The only other documents remaining at Stanford from that year are two, both dated March 1, 1904, signed by the director general of Egyptian museums, who happened at that time to be Emil Brugsch. These documents released six cases of antiquities through customs as being without value to the Cairo Museum.

Among the undocumented acquisitions of Mrs. Stanford's 1904 trip was a cache of scarabs, of which the Museum still retains nearly 150, more than half dating from the Eighteenth and Nineteenth dynasties. Peterson did not catalogue the scarabs until 1917 and when he did, he chalked them all up to Mohammed Ali el Gabri, despite the total absence of scarabs from the dealer's handwritten list. Recently, however, in the course of preparing the present account, a clue to their origin has been found in the memoirs of Archibald H. Sayce, a professor of Assyriology at Oxford at the turn of the century and vice-president of the Egypt Exploration Society. After having spent the better part of forty years on scholarly jaunts to Egypt, Sayce paid a visit to Stanford in 1917. "The rooms of its spacious Museum," he wrote in his *Reminiscences* (1923), "were still a scene of wreckage. The magnificent collection of Greek vases it once contained had been hopelessly shattered; even the Egyptian mummies were torn and dismembered." In the course of evaluating its Egyptian holdings at the request of President Wilbur, Sayce dated the scarabs along with seals, cylinders, and many other objects for Peterson, who was at that time engaged in cataloguing the entire collection. Having studied the group thoughtfully, Sayce wrote: "I discovered among its relics the scarabs which Brugsch Bey had sold many years ago to America, where the European world had lost sight of them, while the Egyptian world invented the scandalous story that they had been abstracted from the Cairo Museum during the Arabi troubles."[99] It would appear that the six cases Brugsch had approved for export contained the wherewithal of a profit-sharing arrangement not unfamiliar to his colleagues in Cairo.

It was one thing, of course, to sell authentic "anteekah" from the nation's patrimony, quite another to palm off outright forgeries. There was so much of this going on, Brugsch wrote to Harry Peterson on another occasion, that he didn't even like to think about it.[100] Yet the Old Kingdom figure of the Seated Cheops (116) that came

85

*117, 118 Two Old Kingdom
reliefs from the false door of
Wedjkaiankhi's tomb at Dashur.*
(SM 66.543,66.544)

back to Palo Alto with Mrs. Stanford in 1904 has been pronounced a forgery by several specialists. Perhaps the creation of one of the skilled Italian or Greek artisans known to have produced sculptures in this style for the rising market of the early twentieth century, the limestone figure has an artfully defaced cartouche on the side of its base that has been deciphered as "Cheops." Nevertheless, according to an account in the *San Francisco Tribune,* May 19, 1904, the figure had been unearthed at Giza "where the pyramids were being explored by a party under the direction of the Sheik" at the very time that Mrs. Stanford was staying at the Ghezirah Palace Hotel in sight of the great pyramids. It is impossible to deduce from the records the identity of the person who succeeded in convincing Mrs. Stanford of this "discovery."

Equally difficult to trace is the name of the dealer who sold her, in 1904, two Old Kingdom reliefs that were genuine (117, 118). Stanford's fragments from the Tomb of Wedjkaiankhi are matched with others in the British Museum, as recognized in 1975 by Charles Van Siclen, an Egyptologist working on the University's collection. Built in the area of Dashur on the west bank of the Nile to the south of Saqqara, the mastaba tomb seems to have been cleared by Maspero between 1881 and 1885, by which time its false door had apparently already been removed. Its upper part was acquired by the British Museum in 1897, its lower by Jane Stanford in 1904.[101]

THE IKEDA COLLECTION

Interspersed with the two trips to Egypt were two trips to Japan, the first in 1902 (119). At that time, Mrs. Stanford added several dozen objects to the collections formed by Charles Delong and Eugene Van Reed in the early 1870s. A few of her purchases came from Kuhn and Kumor, art and curio dealers in Yokohama, others from the shops of Seisuke Ikeda in Kyoto and Tokyo. Among the former were two albums with fifty pictures; among the latter, two bronze lanterns, no longer in the Museum, that were said to have been three hundred years old and to have come from Koyasan, the sacred Buddhist mountain in Kii province. According to turn-of-the-century reports in the San Francisco newspapers, Ikeda had been for many years one of the foremost art connoisseurs in Japan, well-known for his annual collecting trips throughout Asia. His firm, founded in 1861, was a prominent source of art for export from Japan during the last quarter of the nineteenth century.

When Mrs. Stanford returned to the Orient in the spring of 1904, she renewed her aquaintance with the Ikeda family. And two months later, the Ikeda son appeared in San Francisco with a sizable collection of Japanese and Chinese art that he said he hoped to sell to the British Museum. The senior Ikeda had died, leaving a large estate which his widow wanted to use to raise funds for a memorial contribution in his name to the Japanese effort in the war then current with Russia. Hearing of these plans and wanting to foster them and also to acquire Oriental art for the Museum, Mrs. Stanford bought the entire collection for Stanford, paying $27,000 for 418 objects.

Two-thirds of the Ikeda collection was Japanese, comprising sixty-nine paintings (both hanging scrolls and folding screens), sixty pieces of lacquer ware, eighty netsuke, thirty-six porcelains, and a variety of metal objects, mostly sword guards (*tsuba*) and decorative bronzes. Prominent among the forty Japanese paintings now remaining in the Museum is a pair of six-fold screens by the Kanō school of the late-seventeenth century after a Sesshū handscroll in Kyoto (120). Hanging scroll (*kakemono*) paintings include an *Anonymous Rakan*

87

119 (opposite) *Jane Stanford and Bertha Berner in 1902 before the great bronze Buddha known* as the Daibutsu, at Kamakura, south of Yokohama.

120 *One of a pair of six-fold Japanese screens, Edo, Kanō School, late seventeenth to early eighteenth century, based on the* famous Long Landscape *scroll by Sesshū. From the Ikeda collection.* (SM 9005)

88

121 (left) *Yūhi (Kumashiro Shūkō)*, Pea Fowl and Apple Blossoms, *eighteenth century, ink and color on silk. From the Ikeda collection.* (SM 9266)

122 (right) *Nangaku,* Chinese Figures, *1813, ink and color on silk. From the Ikeda collection.* (SM 9247)

123 (below) *Chinese vase (meiping), Qing dynasty, porcelain with underglaze blue and overglaze yellow enamel. From the Ikeda collection.* (SM 9032)

124 *Hokusai,* Woodcutter
Gazing at a Waterfall, *ink and
light colors on paper. From the
Ikeda collection.* (SM 9263)

of the sixteenth century; a *Disciple of Buddha,* eighteenth century, by Kanō Yoshinobu; *Pea Fowl and Apple Blossoms* by Yūhi (Kumashiro Shūko) (121); *Cherry Blossoms with Bees* by Katen; Nangaku's *Chinese Figures,* 1813 (122); and a painting on paper, *Woodcutter Gazing at a Waterfall,* 1798, by Hokusai (124).

The Chinese objects comprised sixty-two ceramics ranging from Han Dynasty green-glazed earthenwares and Song Dynasty Jian *temmoku* tea bowls to late Ming blue and white vases and Qing dynasty porcelains decorated with colorful overglaze enamels (123). There were thirty objects of bronze and other metals, plus twenty-two examples of cloisonné, the earliest dating from the sixteenth century. A rare porcelain vase with peach-bloom glaze that was especially admired by Carl Bishop of the Philadelphia Museum when he examined the Ikeda collection at Stanford in 1917, has long been missing from the Museum. Twenty-nine carvings of jade and other semi-precious stones, lacquers, and woods completed the Chinese holding in the original purchase. Also included were a bronze Buddha figure from Thailand and a gilt bronze figure from Nepal. [102]

The craze for Japanese art that seized the fancy of rich American collectors around 1900 arose partially from the lectures, books, and catalogues of Ernest Fenollosa, first curator (1890–1896) of the first department of Japanese art in an American museum—the Boston Museum of Fine Arts. As a professor of political economy at the University of Tokyo in 1878, Fenollosa began to collect the Japanese paintings that were to constitute the unrivaled collection subsequently given to the Boston Museum by Dr. Charles Weld. A heavily annotated copy of the department's annual report for 1904 is found among the curator's papers at Stanford, a reminder of Jane Stanford's serious interest in Japanese culture.

CONCLUSION

THE STORY OF the Stanford Museum is a variation on the dominant theme of nineteenth-century American museums: interest in the history of man rather than the history of art. Early in the next century aesthetic considerations came to the fore and soon the art museum as we know it today evolved. But in the decades after the Civil War, when travel and income for Americans increased enormously, it was often the ethnographic and the archaeological object that was brought back to fill the museum case. The keynote, as René Brimo noted in a precocious book on the evolution of taste in the United States,[103] was a kind of historical eclecticism. This coloration, which also tinged public museums in Boston, New York, Detroit, Cincinnati, and other cities, was partially the result of the American desire to be in touch with the historical past.

In the formation of university museums, moreover, important elements were the serious study of ethnology, brought into focus by Harvard's Peabody Museum, and of archaeology, first reflected in the American mound relics of the National Museum (Smithsonian Institution). Indeed, university museums preceded public museums in the excavation of the Americas, the Near East, Egypt, and Greece. The University of Pennsylvania, for instance, sent its first expedition to Babylonian sites in 1888 with three others to follow by 1900; Princeton University had an expedition in Syria in 1904; the Reisner expedition to Cairo in 1899, sponsored by Phoebe Hearst for the University of California, was the first American excavation in Egypt, though others by the Metropolitan Museum and the Boston Museum of Fine Arts soon followed. Museums also became the repositories for archaeological and ethnographic collections amassed, like holdings of paintings and sculpture, by private individuals. Jane Stanford's collections, garnered from the Siskiyous to Ceylon, shared the nineteenth century's characteristic commingling of art and artifact with other museums on the East Coast and in the Midwest.

At the Cincinnati Art Museum, established like Stanford's in the 1880s, the founding collection comprised thousands of objects relating to the archaeology of the American Indian and to the arts of Africa. These collections shared Cincinnati's galleries with contemporary paintings by fine regional artists, among them Joseph De Camp, Robert Blum, and Frank Duveneck, much as the Stanford Museum exhibited works by the San Fran-

ciscans Charles Christian Nahl, William Keith, and Thomas Hill. To the Detroit Museum (later the Institute), also founded in the mid-eighties, the head of a local pharmaceutical firm presented a collection of 15,000 ethnographic, archaeological, and Oriental objects, half of which came from Japan alone. Accenting the curious rather than the artistic, the collection was added to holdings of contemporary Academic paintings by both American and French artists and to a sizable collection of Old Masters. The earlier paintings were donated by the founder and publisher of Detroit's *Evening News,* James E. Scripps, a generous donor who later became one of the forty incorporators of the Detroit Museum.

If Detroit had forty incorporators, Stanford had only one, and what was extraordinary about its founder was that Jane Stanford served also as its committee for building, finance, and acquisition as well as presiding as its director and president of its board of governors. Moreover, while the make-up of the Stanford Collection was similar to contemporaneous American museums, the motives for its compilation were unique. For the Leland Stanford Junior Museum was not simply a memorial monument; it was also a shrine containing, together with much else, the ephemera of a boy's life. A consolation for Mrs. Stanford, her preservation of the boy's belongings is a reminder of the Victorian fascination with death and mourning much as her preoccupation with Egyptian art, despite her son's lively interest, suggests a funerary concern reflected also in the sphinxes on the family mausoleum. Cairo itself was a place of mystical fascination where, on a moonlit night in the winter of 1904, Jane Stanford felt so near her loved ones it seemed she could thrust her hands through the stars and "clasp the hands of dear ones longing for [her] to join them."[104] Speculation about her interest in spiritualism, denied during her lifetime, is suggestive. Nor should it surprise us; many of her contemporaries shared this interest just as they subscribed to the anthropomorphizing of the heavenly afterlife. Indeed, "spiritualism is paradoxically the logical façade of materialism," as Ann Douglas writes in her book on nineteenth-century Christian attitudes, *The Feminization of American Culture* (1977).[105]

Until her son's death, Mrs. Stanford had dedicated her considerable energies to his education and to the management, decoration, and furnishing of her various households. As Mrs. Leland Stanford, she unquestionably acted out, from the Pompeian Room on Nob Hill, the ambitious role of social and cultural arbiter in a rough and raw new city. But when her only child, the

125 Leland Stanford Junior
as an Angel Comforting His
Grieving Mother, *1884, by the
French artist Emile Munier,
1810–1895.* (SM 14897)

son born to her late in life, came of age, she removed him from the West and took him to Europe for an education that touched all the great cultural centers, centers with museums and collections she herself had never before seen. This was the beginning of the hegira that kept her away from California for more than half of the next twenty-five years. With the romantic attachment to the ancient past that so affected Americans of her era, she took the boy to Greece and Rome, encouraging him to collect mementos of the classical past. Young Leland responded enthusiastically and, at her urging, began his little collection. But from his letters home, we can see that he was a boy who responded enthusiastically to most of what life offered: soldiers on parade, winemakers in Bordeaux, silk-spinners in Lyons, construction workers on the railroad. War, industry, business, the arts—it is difficult to predict which of a child's adolescent interests will take hold in maturity.

But Mrs. Stanford knew. For with the tragedy of loss came the power of projection. Had he lived he would have continued as a serious collector and given to the people of San Francisco "the grandest museum in the world." In a sense, she was able to control her son's future, to define his profession as work apart from the ruthless, competitive society she had surely come to know. Would there have been a Leland Stanford Junior Museum if the boy had lived? Possibly. But his death made it certain, for death conferred legitimacy on Jane Stanford's ambition to do publicly what she had been doing privately all her life. Moveover, in 1885, when she undertook the museum project, the Stanford campus was a horse ranch covering 8,000 acres of wheat and barley, its hills laced with horse paddocks and dotted with cow barns. The nearest population center was a city thirty-five miles away; the nearest town boasted twenty-seven saloons. The challenge was great. A woman of enormous capability, resolute and courageous, Jane Stanford justified her career—both to herself and to the world—by acting in the name of grieving motherhood. But the Leland Stanford Junior Museum was hers; she built it.

Carol M. Osborne

126 *The Leland Stanford Junior Museum, main facade, designed by Percy and Hamilton, 1891.*

127 *The Glyptothek, Munich, 1815–30, designed by Leo von Klenze.*

128 *The Metropolitan Museum of Art, New York, 1880, designed by Calvert Vaux and J. W. Mould, to which additions were made beginning in 1888.*

The Architectural Significance of the Stanford Museum

THE LELAND STANFORD JUNIOR MUSEUM stands in sharp contrast to the other original buildings of Stanford University. Erected in 1891, at the same time that the Romanesque or Mission-style quadrangles of the University were under construction, the Museum provides an unexpected note of classicism—like a lone toga-clad actor on the stage of a medieval mystery play (126).

Not only is the Stanford Museum distinctive within its immediate context, but it plays a unique role on the larger stage of modern architecture. A new type of museum building was here introduced to America. And a new architectural material, reinforced concrete, was employed in an unprecedented manner. The highly personal motives of the founders of Stanford University, their boldness in planning, and the experimentation of their designers combined to produce a building whose historical significance has never been fully recognized.

NINETEENTH-CENTURY MUSEUM BUILDINGS

In Europe, several structures were erected expressly for the exhibition of art before 1800, such as the Museum Fredericianum in Kassel, built in the 1770s, but it was principally the nineteenth century that produced the museum as a building type.[1] The Glyptothek in Munich (1815–30) (127), the Altes Museum in Berlin (1823–30), and the British Museum in London (1823–47) are among the great buildings that established the architectural form of the modern museum. The United States in the nineteenth century produced only a few significant museum buildings, notably the first Boston Museum of Fine Arts, 1876 (3) and the Metropolitan Museum of New York, begun 1880 (2, 128). Moreover, a survey of European and American art museums before 1890 reveals a stylistic difference between the two groups: the European buildings are normally Neoclassical in form, while the

American ones are nearly all of neo-Gothic, Romanesque, or other nonclassical styles.[2]

The European preference for classicism in museum architecture was not arbitrary. It expressed the circumstances that had given birth to the modern museum, especially the classical scholarship that inspired it, and the collections of ancient art that it often housed. The crown prince of Bavaria, founder of the Munich Glyptothek, specified in 1813 that its architecture should be "purest Grecian," in keeping with the sculpture to be placed in it; even "picture halls," according to the art critic W. H. Wackenroder somewhat earlier "ought to be temples."[3] J. Mordaunt Crook, writing of the British Museum, observed that "etymologically, at least, the modern museum was an attempt to re-create the concept of an antique temple [i.e., 'museum' is literally the temple of the Muses]. Hence the classic format of so much museum design."[4]

But this was fully true only in Europe. It would be interesting to investigate why American museums in the nineteenth century avoided so consistently, almost perversely, the Neoclassicism considered normal across the Atlantic (it can be explained only partly by the stylistic fashions of the decades in which most of the American museums were erected); but this question is beyond the scope of our subject. The important point here is that the Stanford Museum was the first major American museum built in a Neoclassical style.[5] As such, it was the harbinger of the the classicism that finally captivated American museum design in the mid-1890s (part of the general classical revival that swept the country at the time), as seen in the Art Institute of Chicago (1893), the Brooklyn Museum (1895), and the Fifth Avenue façade of New York's Metropolitan Museum (1910). From then on, at least until the triumph of "modern" architecture in the mid-twentieth century, classicism reigned supreme as the ideal for the American museum.

How was it that the Stanford Museum, erected at the farthest remove from European culture, heralded this transformation of American museum design?

BEGINNINGS

The Stanford Museum is, in a sense, older than Stanford University. For its origins are in the collection that the precocious teenager Leland Stanford Junior assembled and displayed in his family's Nob Hill house in San Francisco, and which he hoped to present to the city when it "attained sufficient proportions to rank with other national museums."[6] From 1880 to 1884, the

Stanfords spent the remarkable total of nearly three years in Europe, on two separate trips. Letters and other documents reveal that a major preoccupation of the family during this time was the visiting of museums. Leland Junior's tutor, Herbert C. Nash, later recalled that the boy's favorite leisure activity was museum-going, and that "he had been through half the famous picture galleries of Europe."[7] These included the British Museum, the Louvre, the Belvedere in Vienna, unspecified museums in Rome, Berlin, Frankfort, Marseilles, Genoa, etc.—and, most important for our purposes, the National Archaeological Museum in Athens, which Leland Junior visited shortly before his death in 1884.[8] A story later was told that during this visit, Leland Junior decided to pattern his projected San Francisco museum on the building in Athens.[9] Whether or not this is true, it is a fact that Jane Stanford later used the National Museum of Athens as a model for the building she was planning to realize her son's project.

The National Archaeological Museum of Athens (130)

was the work of at least three architects—two German and one Greek. The original plans were made in 1860 by Ludwig Lange (1808–68); these were revised, first by Panages Kalkos (Παυαγηφ Καλχοφ, 1818–1875) and then by Ernst Ziller (1837–1923), an architect who spent much of his career in Greece.[10] The museum took many years to construct, and in fact was not fully complete when the Stanfords visited in 1884. The severe classical form of the building—with an unpedimented portico of four Ionic columns *in antis,* at the center of the main façade, flanked by long open colonnades, terminating in pedimented blocks at the corners—no doubt was meant to recall the architectural traditions of Greece. But the design principally reflected nineteenth-century Neoclassicism in architecture; and the floor plan of the building—with long rows of galleries forming a square around a courtyard, bisected by a series of rooms on axis with the entrance (131)—was the standard plan that had developed for large museums in Europe, as seen in the Altes Museum in Berlin (132) or the Kunsthistorisches

129 *The entrance façade of the National Archaeological Museum, Athens, 1860–89, designed by* *Ludwig Lange, Panages Kalkos, and Ernst Ziller.*

130 The National Archaeological Museum, Athens.

131 The National Archaeological Museum, Athens, plan.

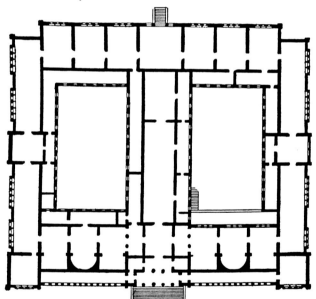

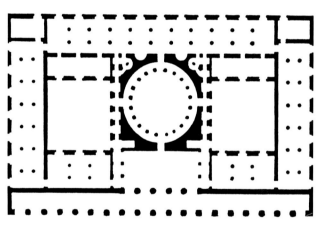

132 The Altes Museum, Berlin, 1823–30, designed by Karl Friedrich Schinkel, plan.

Museum in Vienna.[11] The most distinctive architectural quality of the Athens museum is a stark, almost primitive simplicity (somewhat reminiscent of the work of Claude-Nicolas Ledoux and his avant-garde colleagues of the French Revolutionary period), a quality that the architects of the building may have considered particularly suitable to the newly excavated Mycenaean and Archaic

Greek objects that the museum was intended partly to house.

This was the museum that the fifteen-year-old Leland Stanford Junior visited after exploring the Acropolis, in the snowy January of 1884 in Athens. His tutor later recalled that the celebrated archaeologist Heinrich Schliemann spent part of a day personally going over his collection with the young man, and presenting him with some small objects from Troy for his own museum.

On March 13, 1884, Leland Junior died, in Florence. In their grief, the parents resolved to devote their fortune to a useful memorial to the child; a museum and a university emerged as the favored projects, with Mrs. Stanford taking a special interest in the museum. From the beginning, the university was to be located at the Stanfords' Palo Alto estate, but there was indecision about the site of the Museum. As late as April 1887, with construction of the University's Inner Quad about to begin, Senator Stanford was quoted as saying, "Mrs. Stanford and myself have determined to locate [the] museum in San Francisco," and records in the Boston office of the University's architects, Shepley, Rutan & Coolidge, reveal that they produced designs for a "Museum at Golden Gate Park" for the Stanfords.[12] But the founding grant of the University, written in November of 1885, had specified that "museums" and "galleries of art" were to be included at the institution; Francis A. Walker's planning recommendations to the Stanfords, of November 1886, proposed that a "museum of fine arts" be one of the first twelve facilities erected at the University; and the master plans for the campus produced in 1887 and 1888, by Frederick Law Olmsted and Charles Coolidge, included libraries and museums in the main, north face of the Outer Quad.[13] At the end of 1887, a newspaper story on the University reported that the libraries would be on one side of the great Memorial Arch of the Outer Quad, with the other side devoted to "the natural history and art museum."[14]

In 1889, however, as construction of the Inner Quad proceeded and plans for the Outer Quad were being refined, the architects began to have doubts about including the Museum there. Surviving correspondence between Olmsted in Boston and his on-site representative in Palo Alto, Henry S. Codman, provides some clues to the reasons. In October 1889, Codman discussed several possible sites for "Mrs. S's museum," along the approach to the University (now Palm Drive), noting that some of them were not "large enough for what it will eventually become."[15] Jane Stanford's increasingly ambitious plans for the Museum apparently had outgrown the quads. (Codman even suggested, as one solution, the division of the Museum into two buildings, facing each other across Palm Drive.) And the following April, Codman wrote to Olmsted, "it seems best to keep [the museum] away from the rest, for Mrs. Stanford has certain ideas about it which might not be possible to get properly in harmony with the other buildings."[16]

Surely the most troublesome of these "certain ideas" was Mrs. Stanford's wish to model her building on the National Museum in Athens, a notion she perhaps first mentioned to the architects at this rather late date. A Neoclassical temple, needless to say, could not be inserted into a Romanesque quadrangle without jeopardy to architectural unity. The decision was made to erect the Museum on the west side of the approach to the quads.[17] Mrs. Stanford then chose a San Francisco architectural firm, Percy and Hamilton, to design the building— perhaps because the architects of the Quads were uncooperative or unenthusiastic about its intended form.

Thus, the strong-willed Jane Stanford, guided by personal considerations having to do with her son's activities in the final days of his life, went against the better judgment of distinguished architects, and created a building which introduced a new phase of classicism into American museum architecture. This is not as unlikely as it may seem. Many people assume that the most significant architectural designs result from an architect's complete creative freedom, with the least interference from the client; but architectural history reveals that innovative and important designs are frequently produced for difficult clients with unusual needs or idiosyncratic views. In fact, the Stanford quadrangles themselves are a good example of this phenomenon. Traditionally considered to be the conception of Frederick Law Olmsted, the quads actually resulted from a stormy collaboration between Olmsted and Leland Stanford—a collaboration in which Stanford usually had his way, and in which the most innovative aspects of the design were mainly his contributions.[18] Among these innovations was a degree of monumentality and formal organization new to American campus planning, reflecting European monuments and spaces more than anything to be found in America at the time. The plan of the Stanford quads, indeed, foreshadowed a new type of monumental campus design that was to transform the planning of American universities starting in the 1890s, just as the Stanford Museum foreshadowed the classical transformation of American museums.[19] In both cases, the innovations seem to have sprung from the Stanfords' extensive travels in Europe from 1880 to 1884. Many wealthy Americans, of course, spent time in Europe in the late nineteenth century and returned home wanting to introduce European high culture to America in some way. But the contributions of Leland and Jane Stanford were unique, due to their special motivations, their extraordinary resources, and their willingness to innovate.

133 *The National Academy of*
Science, Athens.

DESIGN AND CONSTRUCTION

Beginning in March 1888, Mrs. Stanford corresponded with individuals in Athens, requesting photographs of the National Museum. Her letters are not known to survive, but some of the replies to them are preserved, and suggest a kind of battle of wills between the correspondents. Mrs. Stanford wrote first to Ernst Ziller, the architect who had produced the final plans for the Athens museum. Ziller seems to have misunderstood—or pretended to misunderstand—which building she wanted to reproduce, and sent her photographs of the Academy of Sciences in Athens, another Neoclassical structure, which he noted he also had designed.[20] He added that if Mrs. Stanford would give him the dimensions of her intended building, he would "have the greatest pleasure to make you the plans of the edifice in a pure Greek style," and stated that it would be "unique in the world." A later exchange of letters with Ziller did not clear up the confusion.[21] In 1890, Mrs. Stanford wrote to Irving J. Manatt, the American consul in Athens, who in October of that year did provide her with photographs of the National Museum, but added, "If I may venture a suggestion now it is that the general plan of the National Museum, with the façade of the Academy, would give

you a structure at once noble and practical for the use in view."[22] Both Ziller and Manatt apparently preferred the more conventional façade of the Academy (less stark and planar than the National Museum), and thought they could mold Mrs. Stanford's plans (133).

But Jane Stanford knew quite well what she wanted. On October 26, 1890, she contacted the San Francisco architects Percy and Hamilton (a terse note from her secretary instructed them to call on her the following day, "on a matter of business").[23] And three days later, she wrote to them as follows:

Sirs, Yesterday I received the enclosed Photos from Athens, Greece. They advise me that interior views could not be had as they are not allowed to be Photoed. I think the style is very like that already adopted at Palo Alto. [This remarkable statement suggests that Mrs. Stanford has attempted to minimize the obvious stylistic differences between the Stanford quadrangles and the Athens Museum, in her previous discussions with Coolidge and Codman.] I also like the center of this [façade]. You might roughly sketch this off for our building—this has a court, as I remember it when there. You will observe among these Photos one of another building, the Academy—which is of another style of architecture but will not do for us. . . . I leave the City tomorrow to be absent until the 5th of November—and I trust on the day following you will have a rough sketch to show me.[24]

George Washington Percy (1847–1900) and F. F. Hamilton (1853–1899), both natives of Maine and trained in architectural offices in New England, had settled in San Francisco about 1876 and joined in partnership in 1880.[25] Although their careers were cut short by early deaths and they are not widely remembered today, in their time they were considered prominent and received important commissions. Their work in San Francisco included the First Unitarian Church on Franklin Street, the Children's Playhouse in Golden Gate Park, the old Academy of Sciences building on Market Street, the Omnibus and Cable Company's buildings, and the Hayward (now Kohl) Building at Montgomery and California streets; among their works elsewhere were the Lick Observatory on Mount Hamilton, the old City Hall in Alameda, an Episcopal church and an insane asylum in Stockton, the Christian Brothers Winery near St. Helena, and Hoitt's School in Menlo Park.[26]

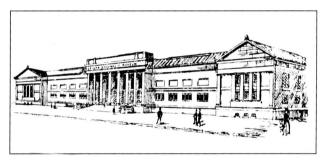

134 *Sketch of design for the Stanford Museum, published in* the San Francisco Chronicle, *January 14, 1891.*

Percy and Hamilton's work prior to the Stanford Museum was largely Richardsonian-Romanesque in style, like the buildings of the Stanford quads designed by Charles Coolidge. So it is unlikely that the Stanfords chose Percy and Hamilton as architects of the Museum, rather than Coolidge, for reasons of architectural style. Mrs. Stanford perhaps wished simply to wipe the slate clean and have architects who would do precisely as she wished. It is also possible that Percy and Hamilton's experience with matters of structure and construction recommended them (a point to which we shall return), especially as Mrs. Stanford wanted the Museum completed very quickly, in time for the scheduled opening of the University in October 1891. Leland Stanford, in particular, must have realized the difficulty of achieving this.

Although Jane Stanford was in charge of planning the Museum, it is clear that her husband kept an eye on the project and advised her on important decisions about it.

Mrs. Stanford's private secretary Bertha Berner gives us a nice insight into how this worked:

Mrs. Stanford undertook [the museum] personally, intending to defray the expenses from her own income. The plans were submitted to her, and she became greatly interested in the work. Mr. Stanford rejoiced in her awakened interest after her long season of quiet grief. Of course the plans were discussed with him, but he made it appear that it depended wholly upon Mrs. Stanford as to what was to be done.[27]

Unfortunately, none of the original architect's drawings for the Museum is known to survive.[28] But written accounts and other sources of information shed some light on the process of design. A story about the proposed building appeared in the *San Francisco Chronicle* in January 1891, accompanied by a rough floor plan and a perspective drawing of the Museum (134)—probably made by a newspaper artist, based on the architect's plans.[29] Except for a few discrepancies, the building was shown as finally constructed. The article noted that "the building has been so designed that at a later period it can be extended so as to form a quadrangle, of which the part now erected will then form only one side." Mrs. Stanford did, in fact, later extend the Museum to create a quadrangle, no doubt as part of her desire to reproduce the Athens museum—which she recalled as having a court, as she noted in her letter to Percy and Hamilton quoted above. But Mrs. Stanford apparently never did acquire actual floor plans of the Athens museum. The quadrangular arrangement of the Stanford Museum as eventually constructed (135) was different from that of the building in Athens; even in the portion erected first, large galleries replaced the series of smaller rooms in the Greek building. Mrs. Stanford evidently gave her architects some freedom in the interior planning of the Museum—except for two rooms (now occupied by the administrative offices), which she specified as replicas of rooms in the family's Nob Hill mansion, to be devoted to Leland Junior's original collections.[30]

But it is clear that Mrs. Stanford instructed Percy and Hamilton to pattern the façade of the Museum closely on the photographs of the Athens museum she gave them. Except for a slight reduction in the length of the Athens building (101 meters or 331 feet long, while the Stanford Museum is 312 feet long), an increase in height to accommodate two floors, and a filling-in of the long open colonnades, the Stanford façade follows its model closely. The open colonnades of the Athens building were replaced at Stanford by windows on the main floor and recessed panels above (into which Mrs. Stanford later inserted mosaics); but the pedimented corner pavilions and the central portico with four Ionic columns *in antis* are nearly identical in the two structures (129).

The really significant contribution of Percy and Hamilton to the Stanford Museum concerned not the building's form (over which they had so little control), but the material of which it was constructed: reinforced concrete. One suspects that Leland Stanford may have anticipated that the building would require special structural expertise, and that this was a reason for hiring Percy and Hamilton as the architects. George Percy (who was the more active member of the firm) had published technical papers on the use of iron and concrete in architecture, and his work included several buildings with unusual structural characteristics, notably the Academy of Sciences in San Francisco (136).[31] Designed in collaboration with the pioneering engineer Ernest L. Ransome (who also joined Percy and Hamilton in the construction of the Stanford Museum), the Academy of Sciences had reinforced-concrete floors that cantilevered beyond cast-iron columns, around an open five-story-high space, creating an impression of lightness and suspension. During construction (which began in 1889), this building's structural safety was questioned by some people, and sections of the floors were subsequently loaded with heavy weights to satisfy the San Francisco building inspectors.[32] This incident may have brought Percy and Hamilton to the attention of the Stanfords.

George Percy later suggested two reasons, economy and speed, for the momentous decision to build the Stanford Museum almost completely of reinforced concrete. (The only major use of another material in the building was the marble facing of the central hall or

99

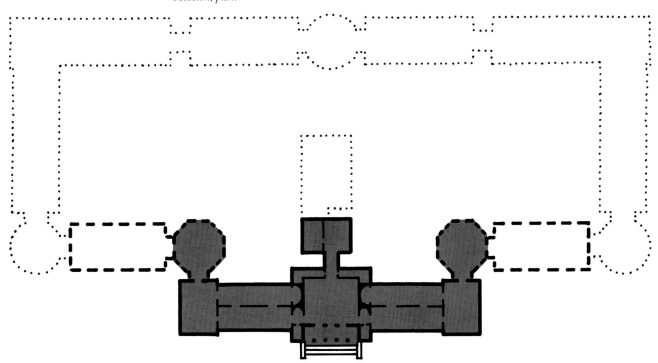

135 The Leland Stanford Junior Museum, plan.

SOLID LINES: Constructed 1891

HEAVY DOTTED LINES: Constructed 1898–99

LIGHT DOTTED LINES: Constructed 1902–06

SHADED AREA: Present museum building

136 *California Academy of Sciences, San Francisco, 1889–91, designed by Percy & Hamilton and Ernest Ransome, interior.*

lobby.) In 1894 Percy stated that the Museum originally was meant to have concrete floors and brick and sandstone walls, but that, "owing to the great cost of stonework," the decision was made to use concrete for the entire structure.[33] Earlier, as the building was nearing completion in September 1891, a newspaper story reported Percy as saying that "he was consulted by Governor Stanford less than a year ago as to a museum building to be completed within the year. He was compelled to confess that with cut stone it was an impossibility. Concrete was then decided upon."[34] Other early stories about the Museum also gave speed of construction as the reason for the use of concrete; this was probably the major consideration.[35]

This is supported by the fact that Percy and Hamilton in 1891 also designed the women's dormitory at Stanford, the first Roble Hall (now Sequoia Hall), and used concrete for it as well (137). Speed of construction was especially important here, as the dormitory had to be finished in time for the opening of the University in October 1891; Percy later recalled that the use of concrete allowed this "three-story building [to be] completed in ninety days from the time the plans were ordered."[36]

In the case of the Museum, there was not the same practical necessity that the building be completed for the opening of the University, but Mrs. Stanford evidently considered this essential, because of the prime importance of the Museum as the fulfillment of Leland Junior's plans. Her resolution in this regard was strong enough to outweigh the reluctance she no doubt felt about constructing the building in a material that many people still considered not respectable.

137 *Roble Hall (now Sequoia Hall), Stanford University, constructed 1891.*

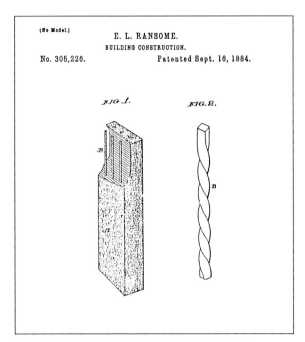

138 Ernest Ransome's twisted iron reinforcing rods, as shown in his patent of 1884.

This is probably the most remarkable aspect of the story of the Stanford Museum—that the Stanfords chose to use a radically new method of construction for the building that was to commemorate their son by embodying the traditions of European high culture. It reveals an ironic combination of conservatism and daring, which can be seen in other ways, too, in the planning of Stanford University. The architectural brilliance of the quads, for example, results in large part from the use of formal, Beaux-Arts principles of planning in thoroughly unconventional ways. Perhaps there is something distinctively American (or Californian?) about this willingness to flout convention while striving to perpetuate tradition.

Concrete had been used in construction by the ancient Romans, but it was not developed as a modern building material until the late nineteenth century.[37] The breakthrough came with the idea of combining the compressive strength of concrete (or "artificial stone," as it was frequently called) with the tensile strength of iron, to produce an excellent material for all architectural elements, including columns, beams, and floor slabs. Starting in the 1870s, experiments were conducted by engineers and architects in France, England, and America, which gradually established the most effective ways of

using this "reinforced" concrete, with iron rods imbedded at optimum points in the concrete. By 1890, the structural potential of the new material was quite well understood, but it was still not widely used, and was normally limited to certain parts of a building, such as floors. Structures totally constructed of concrete were extremely rare, and nearly all were industrial in function. In fact, no public buildings are known—to this author, at least—that were constructed fully of reinforced concrete before the Stanford Museum. (A few public buildings, however, had been erected with walls of *un*reinforced concrete. The principal one, in America, was the Ponce de Leon Hotel in St. Augustine, Florida—where, significantly, Leland and Jane Stanford vacationed, soon after the completion of the hotel, in 1888; this visit may well have made them more favorable to the new material.)[38] Reinforced concrete, which today is used probably more often than any other material in monumental public architecture, was still virtually unknown to it before the Stanford Museum.

Ernest Leslie Ransome (1844–1917), who served as Percy and Hamilton's engineer and contractor for the Stanford Museum, was the foremost innovator in reinforced-concrete technology in America at the end of the nineteenth century. Born in England, of a family involved in early concrete experimentation, Ransome had come to America in the late 1860s and settled in San Francisco, where he made significant improvements in reinforced-concrete design and exploited them in many types of construction.[39] Carl W. Condit has called Ransome "the man who led the way in turning the experimental work [of earlier concrete innovators] into standard building practice."[40] One of Ransome's inventions, patented in 1884 (138), was an iron reinforcing bar of square section, twisted into a spiral form to prevent it from slipping through the concrete (the precursor of the modern reinforcing bar with projections along its surface).[41] Ransome first used his principles in the design of floors, as in the Bourn & Wise Wine Cellar in St. Helena (1888) and the Academy of Sciences in San Francisco, designed with Percy and Hamilton in 1889. At about the same time, Ransome reportedly built the Alameda Borax Works with an entirely reinforced-concrete structure, and constructed the Alvord Lake Bridge in San Francisco's Golden Gate Park, considered to be the first reinforced-concrete bridge.[42] But it was the Stanford Museum that allowed Ransome to apply his innovations fully for the first time.

Engineering journals and other publications reported extensively on the technological significance of the Stan-

ford Museum, both during and after its construction (139).[43] Emphasis was given to the fact that virtually all structural parts of the building were of reinforced concrete—foundations, walls, columns, floors, and even the roof itself, formed of large concrete "tiles" supported on iron trusses. *The American Architect and Building News,* in November 1891, claimed that the Museum was "absolutely fireproof," with no use of wood in it (even the window frames being metal), and that it was "intended also to be earthquake-proof."[44] *The Scientific American* in October 1891 called it "the largest building in the world made of artificial stone."[45] George Percy himself, in *Engineering News* in 1894, suggested that the Museum was "the largest and most important building in the world constructed entirely of concrete," and he pointed out that the forty-six-by-fifty-six-foot roof over the central space, supporting a dome in the center, "is without question the largest horizontal span in concrete to be found anywhere on earth."[46] (Percy noted also that the building contained over 1.1 million cubic feet of space, required about 260,000 cubic feet of concrete, was erected in seven months, and cost about eighteen cents per cubic foot of space—which he stated to be "a very low figure for a thoroughly substantial and fireproof building.")

The curious story, familiar to generations of Stanfordians, that the walls of the Museum contain railway rails, is apparently just a myth. No mention of such members occurs in the accounts of the building's construction, and cuts that have been made into the walls, at various times, have revealed only Ransome's twisted iron reinforcing rods.[47] In fact, the use of massive iron structural members would have been incompatible with Ransome's system of construction, whose advantage lay precisely in its efficient use of small reinforcing rods. The myth may have resulted from a popular misunderstanding, during construction of the Museum or soon thereafter, of the reinforcing system used in the building—a misunderstanding in which Ransome's iron rods were transformed into rails from Leland Stanford's Central Pacific Railroad. If so, this simply underscores the newness and unfamiliarity of Ransome's system at that time.

But Ransome's most significant innovation in the Stanford Museum was probably his treatment of the exterior surface of the building. In 1889 Ransome had taken out a patent for various techniques of handling concrete surfaces (140), which reveal his insights about the future of the material.[48] The appearance of concrete

139 The Stanford Museum in construction.

140 Portion of Ransome's patent of 1889, regarding the treatment of concrete surfaces.

141 The Stanford Museum, detail of exterior surface.

walls did not matter much when they were used simply in warehouses or factories. But Ransome realized that if concrete was to be employed for monumental and public architecture, it was necessary to find alternatives to the irregular and otherwise imperfect surfaces that usually resulted from the wooden forms into which concrete was poured. Ransome's patent of 1889 specified ways in which the form-boards could be constructed so that the resulting concrete wall would have the appearance of masonry blocks, which workmen could then chisel or "bush-hammer" in order to create various textures, similar to those of dressed or rusticated stone. Peter Collins, in his history of concrete, described the significance of this innovation:

> [The Stanford Museum] has the distinction of being probably the first building in which the concrete . . . was tool-dressed to show the texture of the aggregate. The fact that Ransome did this deliberately to imitate masonry is relatively unimportant; of much greater significance is the fact that by removing the thin film of cement which always forms between the aggregate and the form-work, he set a precedent for treating concrete as possessing a natural nobility of its own, instead of regarding it as a cheap infilling or backing. . . . For the first time in the history of architecture, concrete was considered to be the concern of skilled craftsmen, and capable of displaying an inherent beauty.[49]

A close examination of the exterior surface of the Stanford Museum reveals that Ransome actually used the building as a kind of laboratory for the study of this architectural problem (141). Many different techniques for the treatment of concrete surfaces can be distinguished—ranging from the application of a thin coat of smooth cement, to chiseling the surface in order to create a striated effect, bush-hammering to produce a rough surface, and possibly even the use of molds to produce an alternative rustication. Moreover, a pigment was added to the concrete as it was mixed (as is frequently done today, to give concrete an integral color); Percy tells us that this was done in order "to match the sandstone used in the other university buildings."[50] In all these ways, the Stanford Musuem is a milestone in the development of modern architecture. Architects throughout the twentieth century have struggled with the problems of how to handle the surface texture and color of concrete. The Stanford Museum was evidently the first building in the world in which these problems were explored in a comprehensive way.

THE COMPLETED BUILDING AND ITS ADDITIONS

In November 1891 the Stanford Museum was structurally complete, in time for the opening of the university. But work remained to be done, and the dampness of the concrete—which can take some time to dry thoroughly—reportedly delayed the installation of art objects. For various reasons, in fact, the Museum was not finally ready for visitors until about 1894.[51]

By this time, Leland Stanford had died—on June 21, 1893—and Jane had assumed full responsibility for continued construction at the University. The job she faced was overwhelming in its magnitude: most of the Quad buildings were not yet erected, other structures were projected but not yet designed, and ultimately a greater volume of construction at the University was carried out under Mrs. Stanford's direction than under her husband's. It is not surprising that Jane Stanford, lacking Leland's experience in building technology and management, made mistakes. The gravest of these probably was her lack of interest in sound construction practice, which she frequently was willing to sacrifice to superficial architectural appearance. The tragic result was that most of the buildings whose construction Jane Stanford oversaw, following her husband's death, fared poorly in the earthquake of 1906.[52] In fact, the two major buildings she conceived and executed fully on her own—the gymnasium and the library, both erected about 1904–05, on the east side of Palm Drive—were totally destroyed by the earthquake.[53] (It is worth noting here that the gymnasium was strongly Neoclassical in style, and the library was at least semi-classical, which suggests that Mrs. Stanford had an inherent preference for classicism in architecture—a preference which may well have contributed to her original decision to model the Stanford Museum on the National Museum of Athens, rather than to follow the style of the Stanford quadrangles.)

In 1898, Mrs. Stanford began to extend the Museum, in order to produce the quadrangular form she had intended from the beginning. Additions first were built to the north and south, connected to the original structure by rotundas. Percy and Hamilton were retained for the design of these extensions; perhaps to save money, however, they did not consistently employ Ransome's reinforced-concrete system. Their building specifications called for the floors "to be built with Ransome's method of twisted iron and concrete," but the walls were to be of ordinary brick construction (surfaced with a coating of cement "to match the concrete work in [the] old building").[54] The construction firm of Peacock & Butcher submitted the lowest bid for the job, and signed a contract with Mrs. Stanford, on April 20, 1898, agreeing to build the two wings for the remarkably low amount of $39,060, and to complete them in 275 days.[55] At about this time, the façade of the central part of the Museum received the mosaic panels (executed by the Salviati Company of Venice, based on drawings by A. E. Paoletti), which typify Mrs. Stanford's idiosyncratic passion for mosaics; and the two seated statues representing Menander and Faith were placed at the front steps.[56] (Originally, there were also four statues—of Herodotus, Plato, Aristotle, and Plutarch—on the parapet atop the front entrance.)

In 1901–02, the final sections of the Museum were designed by Charles E. Hodges, Mrs. Stanford's resident University architect by then, who also replaced the original low dome over the lobby of the Museum with a high one (which in turn was replaced, after the earthquake, with a dome similar to the original).[57] These wings were constructed from 1902 to 1906, completing the large enclosed quadrangle, and producing a total of two hundred thousand square feet of exhibition space and ninety thousand square feet of storage space—reportedly "the largest private museum in the world" at the time (1).[58] The whole extraordinary complex was thus nearly complete when Jane Stanford died, on February 28, 1905.

One year later, the great earthquake of April 18, 1906, struck the University. Several engineers' reports on the damage were made; one of these, by Edwin Duryea, Jr., noted that the earlier University buildings survived the earthquake well, while the later ones were heavily damaged, and he observed that "the line was so sharply drawn that the main body of the museum, carefully built of reinforced concrete some thirteen years ago, was almost uninjured, while both its wings (lately completed of poorly built brick and stone masonry) were practically ruined."[59] The women's dormitory, Roble Hall—the other building that Percy, Hamilton, and Ransome had constructed at Stanford—also was reported to have survived the earthquake unscathed.

Following the earthquake, the Museum extensions were demolished, with the exception of the two rotundas directly attached to the original portion of the building, and the western side of the quadrangle—whose top floor was partly removed, and which is presently used by the Stanford School of Medicine.[60] This lengthy wing, now standing separate from the Museum, provides striking evidence of the tremendous scale of the fully executed Museum during its brief existence right before the 1906 earthquake.

CONCLUSION

The two principal architectural contributions of the Stanford Museum—its introduction of the Neoclassical museum type to America, and its pioneering use of reinforced concrete—would appear at first to be unrelated. But they may be more than merely coincidental. For reinforced concrete was a particularly appropriate material in which to execute the classical design that Jane Stanford stipulated for her museum. In fact, the National Museum of Athens, with its stark, cubic forms and planar surfaces, looks almost as if it were constructed of concrete itself; these forms and surfaces were unusually well suited to the process by which a reinforced-concrete building was executed. Given the technology available in 1890, the wooden forms into which the concrete was poured could be made to produce simple cubic shapes and flat surfaces much more easily than complex shapes or highly irregular surfaces. (The buildings of the Stanford quadrangles, for example, would have been nearly impossible to execute in concrete.) In the Stanford Museum, the architectural style and the construction technology were neatly appropriate.

To what extent were Percy and Hamilton conscious of this appropriateness? Is it possible that the Neoclassical design presented by Mrs. Stanford actually suggested to them the use of reinforced concrete? One even wonders if Leland Stanford, who frequently had forward-looking insights about architecture, may have been the first to think of concrete as an appropriate material for the Museum. Unfortunately, no evidence regarding these questions is known. It is very likely, however, that Ernest Ransome, once he saw Mrs. Stanford's design, recognized it as a splendid opportunity to explore his new construction system to the fullest.

Thus, the most personal motives of a bereaved mother inspired a building that not only ushered in a new phase of American museum architecture, but facilitated the first monumental use of the principal building material of the twentieth century.

Paul Venable Turner

142 Eadweard Muybridge,
Twisting Somersault, *1879, from*
Attitudes of Animals in Motion,
1881, pl. 106. (SM 13932)

The Stanfords and Photography

FINE PORTRAIT and view photographs, sophisticated viewing equipment, optical toys—all are part of the Stanford Museum's inheritance from the Stanfords. The family was fascinated by photography, one of the marvels of nineteenth-century invention, as was customary for wealthy and imaginative people of the time. For Leland and Jane Stanford, photographs provided visual testimony to their life in California, not only for themselves but also for sharing with relatives in the East.

Among the optical toys—precursors of pictures in motion—are lantern slides in which the image is changed by a movable lever or rack and pinion mechanism, dissolving view lanterns with serial slides for them, and, most importantly, Carlo Ponti's megalethoscope, all now in the Museum's collection. This last-mentioned viewing device was invented and manufactured by the Venetian optician and photographer in the 1860s. The Stanfords bought the custom-made wooden cabinet in Venice in 1883. Slides made of Ponti's photographic prints, pierced in patterns and with translucent, colored drawings laid on the backs, came with the device. By manipulating the various reflective and translucent surfaces of the cabinet, the operator of the megalethoscope could control light from an attached kerosene lamp to produce the effect, in Ponti's *Piazza San Marco* slide, of day fading to twilight, of lamps then appearing in windows, and groups of people promenading in the piazza. The megalethoscope is a diorama for the parlor. The optical toys were bought for Leland Junior, who used the simpler ones but did not live to see the megalethoscope installed in his gallery at home (143).

The portraits and views now in University collections attest to the quality and thoroughness of their photographic commissions. The houses they lived in, telling reflections of their increasing wealth and expressions of their taste in fine and decorative arts, are recorded in three sets of views, each of them rich in historic and aesthetic interest. The first set was made in the mid-1860s by Alfred A. Hart of Sacramento (17), whose photographs of the Central Pacific Railroad of the same period have been highly praised (144).[1] Two sets are the work of Eadweard Muybridge, the photographer then famous for his views of Yosemite Valley and other physical wonders of the West Coast: one set made in 1872 of the Sacramento residence after extensive reconstruction (18–20) and another made in 1878 of the Stanfords' recently completed and furnished Italianate residence on Nob Hill in San Francisco (23–28, 32).

In the 1880s, after the death of their son, Senator and Mrs. Stanford arranged to have photographic progress reports made by Archibald Treat sent to them in Washington so that they could visualize the materialization of the university they were having built in Leland Junior's memory. Treat, who was an ardent and accomplished amateur photographer, produced over three hundred prints of campus sites and buildings as they were being put up in the late 1880s (41).[2]

143 Carlo Ponti's megalethoscope, bought in Venice in 1883, was placed in Leland Stanford Junior's museum room after his death in 1884.

144 Alfred A. Hart, American River and Canyon from Cape Horn, *c. 1864.*

145 Detail of the *Cover of Leland Stanford Junior's* Cahier de Photographies, *c. 1880.* (SM 16797)

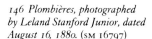

146 Plombières, photographed by Leland Stanford Junior, dated August 16, 1880. (SM 16797)

For portraits of themselves and their immediate family, the Stanfords customarily patronized the best studios, including Bradley and Rulofson, Carleton E. Watkins, G. D. Morse, and Isaiah Taber in San Francisco, and Sarony and Louis Alman in New York. This sort of photographic record was so important to them that every year a portrait was made of Leland Junior sitting in, or standing next to, the plush-covered, fringe-trimmed chairs that were the set pieces of the period's photographic establishments. (See Chronology)

The boy himself became a photographer, one of the few amateurs of the day who went beyond appreciation into practice, and younger than most. In the late 1870s, he had *carte-de-visite* mounts imprinted "Leland Stanford, Jr., Photog., Menlo Park," into which he set the card-sized portraits he made of his aunt Anna Maria Lathrop (91) and of his mother, taken full-length in front of the live oak trees of the Stanfords' Menlo Park estate. His continued interest in the art is represented in a composition book, now in the Museum's collection. He decorated the cover with a drawing of himself standing under a photographer's dark cloth next to the tripod that supported his camera. Its lens is pointed at a French cathedral above which, contrary to the best photographic practice, the sun shines directly at the lens (145). Inside this personal album, which he labeled "Cahier de Photographies à Leland Stanford," the boy pasted large-plate portraits and views he made with his Parisian-bought wet-plate camera. The views are of street scenes and the landscape of Plombières, where he and his mother had stopped for a while in August 1880 (146).

Although the son's practice of photography exceeded custom to a certain extent, the father's use of it, in one particular instance, was so extraordinary that interest in the result was not only familial, or Californian, but international. For Leland Stanford's recognition of photography as a medium that could prove irrefutably an actuality he had observed led to the first stop-motion photographs. The initial subjects of the photographs Stanford commissioned were his fast horses; shortly thereafter the motions of deer, cattle, dogs, oxen, and goats were arrested and, finally, those of men. The photographer was Muybridge (147).

Stanford and Muybridge's collaboration in what they called "photographic experiments" spanned a decade, beginning in Sacramento in 1872 and coming to a troubled conclusion in London in 1882. In 1879, the results of their collaboration were hailed internationally in scientific journals and used by artists in this country and abroad. Stanford's role in the initiation of the photographic analysis of fast motion, widely acclaimed in its time, was subsequently lost to historians of photography, or regarded generally as a matter of local interest. All the acclaim went to Muybridge, and chiefly for the photographic studies made under the auspices of the University of Pennsylvania and published in 1887 as *Animal Locomotion*. In the twentieth century, recognition of Stanford's role jogged along at uneven intervals until a few historians recognized it publicly. Among them was Beaumont Newhall, who honored Stanford in 1954, saying, "it was not an artist, but a horse lover, who pushed photography into the split second, thus opening a new world of vision.[3]

Stanford asked Muybridge to meet him in Sacramento in 1872. By then, Muybridge was the most publicized and ambitious photographer on the West Coast (148). And Stanford at that time was determined to become successful in the breeding and training of fast horses. His interest had been particular at first; experience extended it. As he said in 1890, he

became interested in thoroughbred horses . . . through ill-health. My doctor had ordered a vacation for me and had told me I must go away on a tour. I could not leave at that time. . . . I bought a little horse, that turned out to be remarkably fast, and it was in the using of it that I became interested in the study of the horse and its actions.[4]

That little horse was Occident. It became known, under Stanford's training, as "The California Wonder" (42).

Stanford's study of the horse and its manner of locomotion had been spurred by a controversy among breeders and trainers about whether or not a trotting horse

147 *Eadweard Muybridge by William Vick Studio, Ipswich, c. 1881.*

148 *Muybridge's advertisement on the back of one of his stereographic view cards, c. 1872.* (SM)

had all four feet off the ground at some point in its stride. Sides taken in the argument lined up Eastern against Western horsemen: the former did not believe that there was a moment of unsupported transit; the Westerners did.[5] Stanford even said that he had seen it, but one man's eye was fallible, and his affirmation did not convince. Being a practical man, he sought proof. In 1870, he and Mark Hopkins ran a trotting horse over a smoothed-down sandy track they had prepared and measured the intervals and depths of the impressions of the horse's hooves in an attempt to answer the question. The results were inconclusive. Stanford then turned to the camera.

This was not an original idea. In 1869, Sir John W. F. Herschel, the British astronomer and contributor to photographic processes in the 1830s, had proposed a comprehensive scheme for recording motion accurately and for synthesizing it:

I take for granted nothing more than the possibility of taking a photograph, by a snap-shot—of securing a picture in a tenth of a second of time; and . . . that a mechanism is possible . . . by which a prepared plate may be presented, focussed, impressed, displaced, numbered, secured in the dark, and replaced by another within two- or three-tenths of a second.[6]

Though he regarded his proposal for "the vivid and lifelike reproduction and handing down to the latest posterity of any transaction in real life" as a dream, he believed it to be a realizable one, given time, effort, and money.

Stanford had the last in abundance, and his great interest in the subject made him willing to invest it in a project to prove his point about horses. Such quick work as Herschel envisioned had not yet been done when Stanford summoned Muybridge to Sacramento. The state of the art at that time, particularly the mechanics of shutters and the receptivity to light of the chemicals used, forestalled it. Muybridge dramatized the outcome of Stanford's summons with his usual flair in an article published anonymously in 1881:

Mr. Stanford startled the photographer by stating that what Mr. Stanford desired was a photograph of his horse, Occident. And taken while the horse was at full speed. No wonder even the skilled Government photographer was startled, for at that date the attempts that had ever been made to photograph objects in motion had been made only of the most practicable street scenes. . . . Mr. Muybridge therefore plainly told Mr. Stanford that such a thing had never been heard of; that photography had not yet arrived at any such wonderful perfection as would enable it to depict a trotting horse at speed. The firm, quiet man who had over mountains and deserts and through the malignant jeers of the world, built the railroad declared impossible, simply said: "I think, if you will give your attention to the subject, you will be able to do it, and I want you to try."[7]

Muybridge did try. The first attempt, with Occident as the subject, was shadowy and indistinct. Stanford, however, could read it and to him it was proof of his point. But the indistinct print could not be published. An attempt to get a clearer image of Occident trotting was made the next year. The photograph was evidently circulated, for on April 7, 1873, the *Alta California* called it "a great triumph as a curiosity in photography—a horse's picture taken while going thirty-eight feet in a second." Perhaps Muybridge's indistinct and shadowy proofs were the occasion for the publication in 1873 of the Currier and Ives lithograph *The California Wonder, Occident, owned by Gov. L. Stanford*. The text imprinted on this portrait by the equine artist J. Cameron describes the image as representing "a private trial of speed" (42).

After so promising a beginning, Muybridge's photography of Stanford's fast horse came to a halt. It was interrupted by the troubling circumstances of Muybridge's marriage that eventually led to the death of a San Francisco theater critic and self-described international adventurer, Major Harry Larkyns. In October 1874 Muybridge, believing Larkyns to be the father of the child he had thought his own, shot Larkyns dead in the doorway of the superintendent's cottage at the Yellow Jacket Mine in Calistoga. Muybridge had traveled by steamer and wagon to the mine with a loaded pistol, which he tested with one shot in the air as the team of horses drew him closer to the man who had destroyed his personal life. Muybridge was imprisoned in the Napa County jail; his trial was concluded on February 6, 1875, when the jurors returned a verdict of not guilty. Muybridge's act was judged justifiable homicide; the jury's decision was the last such verdict recorded in a California court. Wirt W. Pendegast, a brilliant young friend of Stanford, was the lawyer whose impassioned two-hour speech swayed the jury. When Pendegast died in 1876, a landslide made it impossible for Stanford's private railroad car to reach the funeral. "I would have given two thousand dollars if I could have looked on the face of Wirt Pendegast again," said Stanford.[8]

The years 1875 and 1876 were also lost to further attempts to improving the quality of Muybridge's photographs of fast motion. Almost immediately after his acquittal, Muybridge made a photographic tour of Central America. But he kept Stanford's commission in mind; during his hours aboard ship, he experimented with new chemicals and a newly devised shutter, which he used in photographing the ship's wake.

Muybridge returned to San Francisco early in 1876. The death of his wife, Flora, and the responsibility for

149 *Eadweard Muybridge,*
Occident Trotting, *1877.*
(SM 13927)

150 *John Koch,* Occident
Trotting, *1877.* (SM 83.48)

the child named Floredo Helios Muybridge occupied him. Printing his Central American work for deluxe presentation albums demanded much of his time, as did photographic commissions. Recovering his position as the preeminent photographer in northern California, he moved to a new studio and announced himself ready to continue his special lines of work: "I am pleased to undertake commissions for the Illustrations of Railroads, Engineering Works, Private Residences, and every description of Landscape and Marine Work and the Copying of Pictures, Drawings, etc. Muybridge, 618 & 620 Clay Street."[9]

Muybridge's skill in copying pictures and drawings was put to Stanford's service in 1877. But it was a strange usage. In that year G. D. Morse of San Francisco

published what Muybridge called an "automatic electro-photograph." It was issued under the title *The Horse in Motion, Illustrated by Muybridge* (149). The subject, again, was "Occident, owned by Leland Stanford; trotting at a 2:30 gait over the Sacramento track, in July 1877." The photograph and the imprinted card were both copyrighted by Muybridge, the first copyrighted material of his work in collaboration with Stanford.

The year in which this photograph was made had long been reckoned as the date from which to calculate centennial celebrations, such was the authority of the pronouncements around its appearance. But in 1972, the published photograph was discovered to be a copy, not of another photograph, but of a painting in the Stanford Museum's collection (150). It is by John Koch, who was regularly employed as a retoucher in Morse's studio. His grisaille painting, in which only the head of the driver is a carefully trimmed and collaged photographic print, was probably made from a lantern-slide projection of a photograph that was indistinct, however automatic and electric the shutter used to snap it might have been. Muybridge rashly described his copy photograph of Koch's painting in a letter to the press: it was "slightly retouched, in accordance with the best photographic practice." The judges of the Twelfth Industrial Exhibition of 1877 weren't troubled by its unphotographic appearance. They awarded this first "Horse in Motion" a medal, "as an illustration of the marvelous resources of photography."

Were the judges aware of the irony of their statement? Probably not. The press, with few exceptions, praised the work. Most likely, Stanford paid it little attention; as before, the original photograph from which Koch had made his painting had been satisfactory enough for him. However fake the photograph, the imprinted card foretold a better future for the experiments in stop-motion photography: an automatic shutter was in use, and with its improvement, the field of instantaneous photography and the revelations it offered would be realized. So sure was Muybridge of his eventual photographic conquest of motion that he added another line to his customary advertisement: "Horses photographed while running or trotting at full speed."[10]

As for Stanford, he determined to expand the photographic experiments and to carry them out at his country estate in Menlo Park, which he had bought in 1876. The *San Francisco Evening Bulletin* of August 3, 1877, reported: "Mr Muybridge intends to take a series of pictures, showing the step of 'Occident' at all stages, and in this manner, for the first time, the precise differences in the motions of different horses can be clearly represented."

This clear representation of animal locomotion had been sought elsewhere in the world, not photographically, but mechanically. Foremost among the researchers was the French physiologist Etienne-Jules Marey (1830–1904; his dates exactly coincide with those of Muybridge). Marey, a professor of natural history at the Collège de France, had devoted his professional life to the study of movement. His method was one of graphic notation derived from a mechanical recording apparatus attached to the moving animal. "There is scarcely any branch of animal mechanics which has given rise to more labor and greater controversy than the question of the paces of the horse," Marey wrote in *La Machine animale, locomotion terrestre et aërienne* (1873). In this work, available in English in 1874 under the title *Animal Mechanism, a Treatise on the Terrestrial and Aerial Locomotion,* Marey described his method and apparatus for recording the motions of the horse:

For the experimental shoe employed in the experiments made on man has been substituted, on the horse, a ball of India rubber filled with horsehair, and attached to the horse's hoof by a contrivance which adapts it to the shoe. . . . When the foot strikes the ground, the India-rubber ball is compressed, and drives a part of the confined air into the registering instruments.[11]

Marey's graphic notations, made of curved and dotted lines and rectangular bars, shaded and solid, were perfectly adequate to scientific inquiry, cool and distant as they were from the full-blooded image of a fast-moving horse (151). Bowing, perhaps, to a desire for the more dramatic image, Marey engaged Emile Duhousset, who also researched the mysteries of animal locomotion, to make drawings of a horse and rider from his graphic notations. A drawing by Duhousset shows the horse at full trot and at the point of its stride when all four feet are clear of the ground (152). The stiffness of the drawing is mitigated a bit by the shadow Duhousset lined in to further demonstrate this unsupported transit. Nevertheless, something was lacking in this representation: the disposition of the horse's limbs, impossible to record by Marey's method, depended on the artist's observation. Even in so experienced a researcher and able an illustrator as Duhousset, the accuracy of this observation could be questioned.

Stanford, according to Muybridge, had read *Animal Mechanism.*[12] Stanford may have paid particular attention to Marey's remarks on the zoötrope, a so-called philosophical toy in which drawings representing successive stages of movement are rotated and viewed through a slotted cylinder, thus making use of the phenomenon of the persistence of vision to create the perception of

151 *Etienne-Jules Marey, synoptical notations of the paces of the horse, from* Animal Mechanism, *1874, fig. 41.*

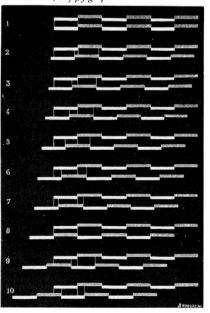

152 *Emile Duhousset,* Horse at Full Trot, *from Etienne-Jules Marey,* Animal Mechanism, *1874, fig. 49.*

continuous movement. Marey suggested a new use for this illusionist toy, usually reserved for the amusement of children: "it has occurred to us that, by depicting on the apparatus figures constructed with care, and representing faithfully the successive attitudes of the body during walking, running, etc., we might reproduce the appearance of the different kinds of progression employed by man."[13] It may be that this reading suggested the next step in the collaborators' studies of motion, for in 1877 Stanford authorized Muybridge to order twelve cameras from the Scovill Manufacturing Company in New York and twelve Dallmeyer lenses from E. & H. T. Anthony Company, suppliers of photographic equipment. It seems clear that in doing so, Stanford had in mind as early as 1877 not only the analysis but also the synthesis of motion. A zoötrope with thirteen slots, the customary number, uses twelve images to convey forward motion. And what more carefully constructed figures might there be than those constructed by photography, which was thought of in the nineteenth century as the very witness of the sun?

In June 1878 the sun shone on what was later called "the motion-picture studio,"[14] a long, white-washed shed facing the track, which held a battery of twelve stereoscopic cameras, placed twenty-one inches apart (153). The cameras faced a screen covered with white cloth, which was marked with vertical white lines, also twenty-one inches apart. The spaces between the lines were numbered from one to twenty in bold black figures at the top of the screen. Another white screen, lower and marked with horizontal lines four inches apart, was placed in front of the tall screen. The first would measure the distance the horse moved as it was photographed serially; the second, how far off the ground its feet were as the camera shutters successively clicked. The track between the white shed and the white screen was covered with powdered lime; as with Stanford's and Hopkins' preparation of 1870, every effort was made to intensify the witness of the sun.

153 *Eadweard Muybridge, general view of the experiment track, 1879, from* Attitudes of Animals in Motion, *1881, pl. F.* (SM 13932)

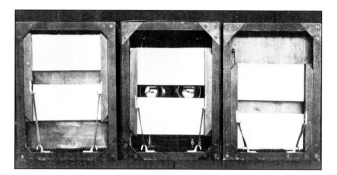

154 *Eadweard Muybridge, electro shutters, with positions of panels before, during, and after exposure, 1879, from* Attitudes of Animals in Motion, *1881, pl. C.* (SM)

The "automatic-electro" shutter system that Muybridge had announced in 1877 was in place. On each camera, a slide with an open slit was placed in front of the lens, forming a shutter (154). Each shutter was connected with a wire that ran across the track in alignment with the verticals on the high white screen opposite. These wires ran underground to a point about two feet from the background screen, then above the ground, where the wheels of the sulky drawn by a trotting horse would close the circuit and trip each shutter in succession. Thus, a measured series of twelve photographs would be made. For photographing running horses, fine threads were strung breast-high across the track at the same twenty-one inch interval and similarly connected to the shutters.

This electrical system, based on a model Muybridge submitted, was contrived with the help of men from the shops of the Central Pacific Railroad and of other San Francisco electricians: Arthur Brown, John D. Isaacs, and Paul Seiler. It replaced Muybridge's first device, a mechanical clock, which didn't work. He tells the story himself in an account of the setup published in the *San Francisco Morning Call,* June 16, 1878:

His [Muybridge's] first endeavor was to open the slide of the camera by hand as the horse went by, but this was too slow to give a clear picture; and then a machine was made which would run at a regular rate, and which could be graded to the speed of the horse. This was a very ingenious contrivance, in appearance between a clock and a music box, but the difficulty was to regulate the horse with the machine.... This machine had to be started by hand, so that there were two uncertain elements to interfere. Could electricity be used, and the current controlled at exactly the right moment, the difficulty would be overcome. When Governor Stanford drove the last spike which connected the Union and Central Pacific Railways, and in a

figurative sense united the Atlantic and Pacific Oceans, though the broadest part of the continent intervened, the blow of the hammer was echoed by a salvo of artillery from the shores of the bay. The act itself was the herald which announced the completion of the great design; and surely, if it could thus be drove across mountains and valleys, the same agency [i.e., electricity] would solve this portion of the problem. But it required a large outlay to perfect the machinery, and involved the sending for a portion of the work from England. It also required time; but the idea, once entertained, could not be abandoned, and the delay only intensined [sic] the purpose to carry it to a successful termination.[15]

So assured was he of a successful outcome that Stanford invited representatives of the local press to the Palo Alto Stock Farm to watch the making of the stop-motion photographs. His horse Abe Edgington was driven by the trainer Charles Marvin past the battery of cameras. As Edgington "came down the track in splendid style, with a good square motion and a firm trot . . . the sound of the slides [shutters] closing was like a continuous roll, so quickly was the feat accomplished."[16]

The racing mare Sallie Gardner then "rushed down the track like a whirlwind," breaking the breast-high threads and tripping the cameras' shutters as she progressed. Other stars of the 1878 serial photographs were Mahomet, who cantered at an 8:00 gait, and Occident, who trotted at a 2:20 gait. Muybridge calculated the exposures at "about 1/2000" of a second or less. Photographic instantaneity, which Herschel had dreamed of in 1869 as a snapshot made in a tenth of a second, was finally achieved in a fraction of that time at the Palo Alto Stock Farm.

The press praised Stanford and Muybridge for their respective parts in the achievement: Stanford for his conception and financial support of the experiments; Muybridge for his ingenuity in completing them. "It is difficult to say to whom we should award the greater praise," was how the reporter for the *Pacific Rural Press* put it. Eyewitness accounts were published in California papers and, on July 27, 1878, copied in a brief notice in *Scientific American*. In October, after prints of the photographs had been received, *Scientific American* devoted its cover to reproductions of them, and published an article entitled "The Science of the Horse's Motion," which was illustrated by line drawings made from Muybridge's photographs. In all quarters, the photographs were received as the truth correcting the vague impressions of human observation.

By August, Muybridge copyrighted and published a set of six photographs, each illustrating a different stride of Stanford's horses. He titled the set *The Horse in*

Motion, Illustrated by Muybridge (46), and sold them for $2.50 each. The French publication was titled *Les Allures du Cheval;* the German, *Das Pferd in Bewegung.*

Between June 1878 and summer 1879, twelve more cameras and pairs of lenses were ordered, and the photographic setup was expanded to accommodate them. Letters arrived from artists, students of anatomy, horsemen, and others urging continuation of the project. "A lecturer on anatomy in an art school," reported the *Alta California* on November 21, "wants a series showing the changes in position of the muscles while running, thus supplying a great want of art students." Most likely this was the painter Thomas Eakins, with whom Muybridge is known to have corresponded in 1879.

Perhaps the greatest incentive to continue, especially for Muybridge, came from Paris. There, Gaston Tissandier, editor of the journal *La Nature,* had published the results of Marey's investigations of animal locomotion in late September and early October 1878. In December, he published copies of Muybridge's *The Horse in Motion.*[17] Marey was quick to respond. On December 18, he wrote to Tissandier:

I am impressed with Mr. Muybridge's photographs published in the issue before last of *La Nature.* Could you put me in touch with the author? I would like his assistance in the solution of certain problems of physiology too difficult to resolve by other methods. For instance, on the question of birds in flight, I have devised a kind of photographic revolver [*fusil photographique*] for seizing the bird in . . . a series of attitudes that impart the successive phases of the wings' movement. . . . It would clearly be an easy experiment for Mr. Muybridge. Then what beautiful zootropes he could make. One could see all imaginable animals during their true movements; it would be animated zoology. So far as artists are concerned, it would create a revolution for them, since one could furnish them with true attitudes of movement; positions of the body during unstable balances in which a model would find it impossible to pose.[18]

Marey concluded, "my enthusiasm is overflowing; please respond quickly. I'm behind you all the way." With this response from an eminent physiologist who had studied the subject for almost twenty years, the photographs produced at Palo Alto took on the aspect of a major contribution to contemporary scientific inquiry. And with this direct address from Marey, Muybridge took to himself the role of international spokesman for the experiments. He responded to Tissandier in February 1879, asking him to tell Marey that his *Animal Mechanism* had inspired Leland Stanford to use photography to investigate animal locomotion. As for photographs of the flights of birds, Muybridge foresaw greater difficulty in getting satisfactory results than with terrestrial subjects

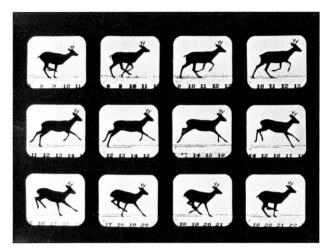

155 *Eadweard Muybridge,* Deer Trotting, *1879, from* Attitudes of Animals in Motion, *1881, pl. 86.* (SM)

but promised that "we will set about it as best we can." Through an agent in Paris, he sent a set of photographs of 1878 to Marey, with his compliments.

The following summer, dogs, deer, cattle, goats, and oxen moved as fast as they could past Muybridge's cameras (155). Muybridge made more stop-motion photographs of Stanford's horses (156). And, in August, man performed on Muybridge's motion-picture stage (157). Stanford's secretary, Frank Shay, had invited the athletes of San Francisco's Olympic Club to show their gymnastic prowess before the cameras.[19] Among the successful results was a series of photographs of Mr. Lawton turning a somersault (142). The athletes also posed in "classical groupings" as the *San Francisco Chronicle* called their body-juggling acts on August 9. The newspaper reported that "Governor Stanford will have each negative worked up to a cabinet-sized photograph, and take one of each with him to Europe, where he will have two life-size oil paintings made of each."

156 *(overleaf, p. 116) Eadweard Muybridge,* Mahomet Cantering, *series of six and series of twelve, 1878;* Mahomet Running, *1879;* Sallie G. Running, *1878;* Frankie Leaping, *1879;* Mahomet Running, *1879; from* Attitudes of Animals in Motion, *1881, pls. 16, 18, 37, 43, 53, 149–50.* (SM)

157 *(overleaf, p. 117) Eadweard Muybridge, from the* Athletes *series, 1879:* Running, Running High Leap, Flip-flap, Swinging Pick *(the model is Muybridge),* Posturing, Running, *and* Walking, *from* Attitudes of Animals in Motion, *1881, pls. 95, 103, 109, 110, 115, and 192–93.* (SM)

By the end of the summer's work, Muybridge had introduced a new twist to his method, at the suggestion of a local artist. He took synchronized views of both men and horses from four or five different positions. His name for them, "foreshortenings," suggests the artistic use for which he designed them. This method was basic to Muybridge's later work at the University of Pennsylvania.

Marey was not alone in foreseeing "beautiful zoötropes." Stanford, as we know, had provided for the future use of the stop-motion photographs in a zoötrope by his determination to set up a battery of cameras, first twelve, then twenty-four. The editor of *Scientific American* had also proposed using the photographs in that cylindrical device that, when whirled, produces the appearance of animated figures. And Thomas Eakins, working with Muybridge's photographs, had plotted the positions of the various parts of the horses' bodies and made diagrams of their movements from the beginning of one stride to the start of the next. Dividing the stride into twelve parts, he then drew the horse in those twelve successive positions. According to Fairman Rogers of Philadelphia, who reported this in *The Art Interchange* on July 9, 1879, "When the figures thus made are put into the zoötrope, a perfect representation of the motion is obtained . . . [it] is exceedingly smooth, and such things as the waving of the tail or the mane are shown in the most natural manner." Rogers concluded his discussion of the difference between customary representations of horses in motion and the attitudes shown in photographs with thanks to Muybridge "for the valuable addition he has made to the general fund of knowledge."

The next, and most spectacular, step was Muybridge's. At Stanford's urging, he devised an instrument that not only animated zoology, but projected it as well.[20] This was a combination of existing instruments, the magic lantern and the phenakistoscope. Muybridge first called his viewing machine, by which he projected copies from the photographs to life-size with brilliant light from an oxyhydrogen lamp, the zoögyroscope. Later, he settled on the name zoöpraxiscope. "By it," he said, "wisdom was at last justified of her children."[21]

The zoöpraxiscope was, Muybridge said twenty years later, "the first apparatus ever used, or constructed for synthetically demonstrating movements analytically photographed from life, and in its resulting effects is the prototype of all the various instruments which, under a variety of names, are used for a similar purpose today."[22]

The first audience for the first moving pictures taken from life was Leland Stanford, who saw them in the

158 *Eadweard Muybridge,* Phases of the Eclipse of the Sun, *January 11, 1880.* (SM 13920)

parlor of his home on the Palo Alto Stock Farm in autumn of 1879:

Across the great screen again and again galloped at full speed a delicate-limbed race mare. Mr. Stanford looked at it. "That is Phyrne Lewis," said Mr. Muybridge. "You are mistaken," said Mr. Stanford; "I know the gait too well. That is Florence Anderson." The artist was certain it was Phyrne Lewis. Mr. Stanford was equally certain it was Florence Anderson, and it was only after investigation and the discovery that by a misunderstanding it was the pictures of Florence Anderson that had been done in silhouette that the artist was convinced of his error.[23]

Muybridge gave a zoöpraxigraphical lecture to members of the San Francisco Art Association on May 4, 1880. Public enthusiasm for the demonstrated synthesis of analytically photographed motion was confirmed in newspaper reports. "Nothing was wanting but the clatter of hoofs upon the turf," the *San Francisco Call* reported the next day. *Alta California,* whose publisher, Frederick McCrellish, had been privy to the Stanford-Muybridge collaboration since its beginnings,[24] now prophesied: "Mr. Muybridge has laid the foundation of a new method of entertaining the people, and we predict that his instantaneous, photographic, magic-lantern zoetrope will make the rounds of the civilized world."

The prophecy was accurate, nearly. But between showing his pictures in motion to Stanford in 1879 and setting out to conquer the world in 1881, there was work to be done in California. First, Muybridge made and published serial photographs for Stanford of the eclipse of the sun on January 11, 1880, the last of his Palo Alto commissions, and the last such photographs made with the by-then outdated wet-collodion method (158).[25] Muybridge was also giving lectures in California, in which he took over from Stanford the analysis of the gaits of the horses he had photographed, increasingly comparing his photographs with examples of the "wrong" representation of the horse in art from the time of the Egyptians, a notion he had gotten from Marey's and Duhousset's publications. As part of the concluding stage of his photographic research for Stanford, he wrote his dramatic account of the years of collaborative effort in which the two of them had been engaged.

By this time, Stanford was planning to publish a book on animal locomotion as it had been revealed in Muybridge's photographs. Muybridge's version of the history, from which excerpts have been quoted above, was published in the *San Francisco Examiner* in February 1881, under the title "Leland Stanford's Gift to Science and to Art." He believed that this was to serve as an appendix to the text of Stanford's book, which was to be written by Dr. Jakob Davis Babcock Stillman, a '49er and a friend and associate of Stanford from his early days in Sacramento.

Finally, Muybridge printed at least eight copies of the 203 photographs that make up, with a printed introductory text and index, that rare volume he titled *The Attitudes of Animals in Motion*. This summation of his work for Stanford was published in Menlo Park in May 1881 and copyrighted by Muybridge. He presented a copy to Stanford, in which the following was imprinted: "Hon. Leland Stanford: Sir—Herewith please find the photographs illustrating *The Attitudes of Animals in Motion,* executed by me according to your instructions, at Palo Alto in 1878 and 1879. Muybridge, Menlo Park, 15th May, 1881."[26]

Muybridge arrived in Paris in September 1881. The Stanfords, who had sailed in 1880 for their first tour of the continent, were already there. Stanford had visited the painter Meissonier and was sitting for the portrait, now in the Stanford Museum, that Meissonier completed in July 1881 (56). According to an eyewitness account published in the *Sacramento Daily Record-Union,* the millionaire did not win Meissonier's favor until he convinced the painter, famous for his paintings and drawings of horses in motion, that he had participated in the photographic studies of which he showed a number of prints. Meissonier looked at the photographs of galloping horses with incredulity; if they represented reality, his life's work was wrong. It could not be so, he said. "The machine cannot lie," replied Stanford.[27] Meissonier's portrait includes a copy of Muybridge's *Attitudes.* Like Stanford's cane, which was bound in gold from a California mine, the book that contained the astonishing

photographs of motion became one of his identifying attributes.

While Stanford was sitting for Meissonier, Muybridge was meeting with Marey. On September 26, in Marey's home in Paris, he showed his serial photographs set in motion in the zoöpraxiscope before an audience of European scientists. In describing Muybridge's demonstration, the scientists abandoned their customary precision; they had seen a *"chasse infernal"* and a *"défilé diabolique."*[28] Two months later, on November 26, Muybridge was at Meissonier's home. The artist had prepared a reception for him, to which he invited two hundred eminent members of the artistic and literary worlds of the French capital. In reporting on this "magnificent entertainment," the *American Register* noted that "the various positions of the horse and the dog, many of which, when viewed singly, are singular in the extreme, were at once resolved into the graceful, undulating movements we are accustomed to associate with the action of these animals."[29]

Stanford was not in the crowd at Meissonier's reception. Whether or not he was invited, he and Mrs. Stanford left Paris on the same day; Muybridge saw them off at the railroad station. Two days later, in a letter to Frank Shay, Stanford's secretary on the Palo Alto Stock Farm, Muybridge commented that "the Govs. health left much to be desired. . . . His residence in Paris has been entirely devoid of pleasure, both to himself and to Mrs. Stanford." While ill-health must have accounted for Stanford's lack of pleasure, one also senses the possibility of his dismay at the public's lionization of Muybridge following his dramatic presentation of the Palo Alto material. The contrast between Stanford's customary reserve and Muybridge's flamboyant showmanship, suppressed when there was work at hand, must have been increasingly evident to both men during Muybridge's Paris sojourn.

Moreover, Muybridge had evidently petitioned Stanford to continue the photographic experiments. He argued that they would be better than those of 1878 and 1879, now that he knew of the faster dry-plate process. But Stanford must have refused, for Muybridge also informed Shay that he would soon visit England to call on "some wealthy gentleman," to whom he had letters of introduction, "to provide the necessary funds for pursuing and indeed *completing* the investigations of animal motion." Muybridge may have hoped that his underscoring of "completing" would bait Stanford, but the Governor did not bite.[30] In a subsequent letter to Shay, Muybridge spoke of a possible collaboration between himself, Marey, and Meissonier. It was to be supported by a wealthy friend of the painter, and would be "a new series of investigations which I intend shall throw all those executed at Palo Alto altogether in the shade."

The project was a confused one, as Muybridge described it. Meissonier would be editor and publisher. The book would include new photographs by Muybridge and its subject would be "the attitudes of animals in motion as illustrated by both ancient and modern artists." The role of Marey is unclear; the "capitalist" was never named. Perhaps he was a fiction, for Muybridge continued:

Both [Meissonier] and I considered it appropriate to invite the Governor to join us if he is so disposed, which we have done by letters. We shall be pleased to welcome him if he is inclined to come in, if he declines, we will avail ourselves of the desire of M. Meissonier's friend.[31]

Stanford made no reply, either to this suggestion or to Muybridge's inquiry about his desire to acquire American copyrights for the photographs, which Muybridge then held. As for joining the new venture, why should Stanford support something that would put the Palo Alto work, made under his auspices, at his farm, and with his horses, "entirely in the shade"? That earlier work had been entirely satisfactory to him. In fact, at that time his own book based on the serial photographs was close to publication; all 2,000 copies of the first edition would be off the press by the middle of the next January.[32]

Muybridge moved to London in March 1882; apparently the connection with Meissonier's mysterious capitalist friend had failed. His success before audiences at the Royal Institution, which included "the coming King and Queen, their children and their brother, the Dukes of Westminster, Sutherland, Argyll, and Richmond . . . Sir Frederick Leighton, Professors Tyndall, Gladstone, and Huxley, and the poet laureate, Alfred Tennyson" was widely publicized.[33] The audience responded throughout the lecture with "a warmth that was as hearty as it was spontaneous."[34] At a demonstration before members of the Royal Academy, Alma-Tadema was enthusiastic in his praise. Sir Frederick Leighton, chairman of the meeting, thanked Muybridge for the new information he had provided the artists of the academy.[35] The brilliant critic, George Augustus Sala, defined Muybridge's zoöpraxiscope as "a Magic Lantern Run Mad (with method in its madness)," adding "had Muybridge exhibited his 'Zoopraxiscope' three hundred years ago, he would have been burnt for a wizard."[36]

During these triumphs, Stanford's name was seldom

mentioned. Nevertheless, Muybridge kept his projected book very much in mind. In March, the photographer wrote a jaunty letter to Dr. Stillman, inquiring after the progress of his text for Stanford's book:

You are I suppose still writing away; you perhaps recollect what I originally told you about the time it would take; and if you succeed in getting the work in the market before 1883, I shall consider you fortunate. Who have you arranged with to publish it?[37]

In the same letter, Muybridge offered to share his most recent information with the doctor, to be worked up "for our joint benefit." He supposed, furthermore, that his photographs were not to be used as illustrations in the book, since he had not heard from Stanford about permission for use and Muybridge still held the copyright. Despite the bravado, one senses that Muybridge had got wind of what was going on in far-off California, and he wanted to receive information, rather more than he wished to give it.

In fact, Stanford's book was already off the press, carrying the full title *The Horse in Motion, As Shown by Instantaneous Photography, With a Study on Animal Mechanics, Founded on Anatomy and the Revelations of the Camera, in which is Demonstrated the Theory of Quadruped Locomotion,* by J. D. B. Stillman, A.M., M.D. Its publisher, in answer to Muybridge's question, was James R. Osgood of Boston, who in the 1870s could list Tennyson, Harriet Beecher Stowe, and Oliver Wendell Holmes among its authors. Stanford had left the preparation of the text, the plates, the binding, and even the title completely to Stillman. But he himself wrote the preface. The book reached London in April, and an extract of Stanford's preface was printed in *Nature* (London) on April 20. It showed, the editor said, "the exact part taken by each of those concerned in the investigation." Because his preface is Leland Stanford's considered public account of the experiments, it is given here in full:

I have for a long time entertained the opinion that the accepted theory of the relative positions of the feet of horses in rapid motion was erroneous. I also believed that the camera could be utilized to demonstrate that fact, and by instantaneous pictures show the actual position of the limbs at each instant of the stride. Under this conviction I employed Mr. Muybridge, a very skillful photographer, to institute a series of experiments to that end. Beginning with one, the number of cameras was afterwards increased to twenty-four, by which means as many views were taken of the progressive movements of the horse. The time occupied in taking each of these views is calculated to be not more than the five-thousandth part of a second. The method adopted is described in the Appendix to this volume.

When these experiments were made it was not contemplated to publish the results; but the facts revealed seemed so important that I

159 *Eadweard Muybridge,*
Mahomet Running, *1879, from*
Attitudes of Animals in Motion,
1881, pls. 141. (SM 13932)

160 *After Muybridge's
photograph,* Illustration of the
Paces, Rapid Walking, *from* The
Horse in Motion *by J. D. B.
Stillman, 1882, pl. 75.*

determined to have a careful analysis made of them. For this purpose it was necessary to review the whole subject of the locomotive machinery of the horse. I employed Dr. J. D. B. Stillman, whom I believed capable of the undertaking. The result has been that much instructive information on the mechanism of the horse has been revealed, which is believed to be new and of sufficient importance to be preserved and published.

The Horse in Motion is the title chosen for the book; for the reason that it was the interest felt in the action of that animal that led to the experiments, the results of which are here published, though the interest wakened led to similar investigations on the paces and movements of other animals. It will be seen that the same law governs the movements of most other quadrupeds, and it must be determined by their anatomical structure.

The facts demonstrated cannot fail, it would seem, to modify the opinions generally entertained by many, and, as they become more generally known, to have their influence on art.

On the basis of this description of him as only a skilled photographer employed by Stanford, a monograph that Muybridge had prepared for the "Proceedings" of the Royal Institution was rejected. His promising career in London cut short, and his sense of justice outraged, Muybridge immediately replied (April 27, 1882):

Will you permit me to say, if the quoted "extract" from Mr. Stanford's preface is suffered to pass uncontradicted, it will do me a great injustice and irreparable injury. At the suggestion of a gentleman, now residing in San Francisco, Mr. Stanford asked me if it was possible to photograph a favorite horse of his at full speed. I invented the means employed, submitted the result to Mr. Stanford, and

accomplished the work for his private gratification, without remuneration. I subsequently suggested, invented, and patented the more elaborate system of investigation, Mr. Stanford paying the actual necessary disbursements, *exclusive* of the value of my time, or my personal expenses. I patented the apparatus and copyrighted the resulting photographs for my own exclusive benefit. Upon completion of the work Mr. Stanford presented me with the apparatus. Never having asked or received any payment for the photographs, other than as mentioned, I accepted this as a voluntary gift; the apparatus under my patents being worthless for use to anyone but myself. These are the facts; and on the bases of these I am preparing to assert my rights.

Muybridge hurried back to the United States to assert his rights. In July, he advised James R. Osgood Company of his intention to sue. In *Muybridge vs. Osgood,* he sued for the infringement of his rights in the use of his copyrighted photographs as the basis for the lithographic illustrations published in *The Horse in Motion.* Muybridge said that the agreed-upon title of the book was to have been *The Horse in Motion as demonstrated by a series of photographs by Muybridge with an attempt to elucidate the theory of animal locomotion by J. D. B. Stillman published under the auspices of Leland Stanford,* and asked for the court to restrain Osgood from selling the book, for unsold copies to be surrendered to him, and for the defendant to pay the cost of his suit.[38]

No doubt Stillman disdained the unfortunate locution Muybridge had used to describe his study. When he heard about Muybridge's suit in April, he immediately wrote a lengthy defense of his and Stanford's position. From Stillman's letter we learn that Muybridge had left his photographs with Stillman for use in the book. But it was in Muybridge's mind to be a very different sort of publication; for him, it was to be "a monument to [Stanford's] farm, like Audibon's [sic] work on ornithology." That is, Muybridge wanted a publication in which his photographs were reproduced with as much care as Audubon's drawings had been, as big and as beautiful. Instead, most of his photographs had been reduced to line drawings (159, 160). We also learn that Muybridge had suggested that the book be produced in England because he didn't believe it could be done well in the United States. Stanford, however, wanted the work done here, "in his own country, where the experiments had been made."[39]

When the *Muybridge vs. Osgood* suit was heard in Massachusetts, the defendant responded that the proprietor, the "sole owner," of the book was Stanford. The suit was dismissed without trial. Muybridge then instituted *Muybridge vs. Stanford.*

After hearing the details of Muybridge's suit against him, Stanford described them in a letter to Stillman:

Muybridge [charges] that I have, by the publication of the book, injured his professional reputation. He wants damages to the extent of $50,000, and claims that the idea of taking photographs of the horses in motion originated with him, and not with me, and that I set up that claim in the book.

When I first spoke to Muybridge about the matter, he said it could not be done. I insisted, and he made his trials. He has often stated this to others, and I think there will be no difficulty in deflating his suit. . . . I think the fame we have given him has turned his head.[40]

And later, Stanford told Stillman that he wanted to "prove up the whole history. The actual facts are from the beginning to the end he was an instrument to carry out my ideas."[41] Muybridge lost his suit on February 13, 1885. The testimony of John D. Isaacs, whom Stanford had employed to make the automatic shutters work, was instrumental in overcoming Muybridge's claims to complete authority in the production of the serial photographs.

Years later, in the draft of a letter to Stanford, Muybridge set forth his case all over again, mentioning a letter to Stanford of August 7, 1877, in which he had suggested "a plan for making a series of electro-photographs, automatically, by which the consecutive phases of a single stride could be successfully photographed." He wrote this, he said, "in justice to both you and myself." The letter of 1877 has never been found; if the drafted letter was sent, there is no known reply.[42]

As for the book, Stanford's only venture in publishing, there had been trouble with it since its inception. Stillman, whom Stanford had invited to write the text and oversee its production, was a specialist in neither the anatomy of the horse nor the production of books. In November 1882, William R. French, brother of the sculptor Daniel Chester French (and later director of the Chicago Art Institute) made a list of errors, discrepancies, and controversial statements he found in *The Horse in Motion.* He sent the list to Stanford with a gracious letter expressing his hope that it would be useful and adding, "My brother . . . has been modelling an equestrian statue (Paul Revere, for Boston) and has used your book."[43]

But the text, according to French's notes, was less readily put to use. His criticisms of page 39 are typical of his notes on Stillman's work: "A difficult passage. . . . There are several errors in the references of the plates, and much confusion of the muscles with each other in the text, so that half a dozen readings are necessary for its comprehension. . . . It ought to be recast." Stillman marked on French's manuscript, "the writer disclaims any design of writing a complete treatise on anatomy."

A lengthy and frequent correspondence between Stillman in San Bernardino, California, and the publisher Osgood in Boston details the difficulties of the book's production. Duplicate chromolitho plates, which required ten separate printings, had been approved by Stillman; color plate 9 had no reference letters on it, although it was referred to by letters in the text. Moreover, Stillman led Osgood to believe that Stanford would order a large number of copies, but he asked for only twenty-five.[44]

Finally, the book did not sell. "What is to be done about the future of the book?" Osgood asked Stillman in 1883, when Muybridge's suit against Stanford was in process. "It has almost entirely stopped selling, and we know of no way to galvanize it."[45] There didn't seem to be a way. Stanford advised Stillman, "Don't allow the matter to worry you. If the people don't buy the book it

Leland Stanford Jr, on his pony Palo. Alto. May 1879

photographed. May 1879 by Eadweard Muybridge

a series of 8 phases of a stride by a pony while cantering. Photographed on wet collodion plates. E.M.

161 Eadweard Muybridge,
Leland Stanford Junior on His
Pony, *1879, from a set of eight*
lantern slides. (SM)

is their misfortune as well as ours. As a money matter, if I am not called upon to pay more, it is of the past."[46]

And so Stanford's *Horse in Motion* came to rest, while Muybridge's photographic investigation of animal locomotion was continued at the University of Pennsylvania. In his publication of that work, *Animal Locomotion* (1887), he cited its beginnings in Palo Alto. In his two subsequent publications, he added this line to the title page: "Commenced 1872. Completed 1885."

⚜

The photographs commissioned by the Stanfords have found suitable places in the University and various uses

by historians and others, but none of them have been more frequently sought out than the Muybridge serial photographs. Harry C. Peterson, curator of the Stanford Museum from 1900 to 1917, noted an early use: "Given out or loaned as follows. May 25th 1900—by order from Mr. Hodges—one small book entitled 'Attitudes of Animals in Motion,' was loaned to R. Schmidt, the sculptor, for guidance in modeling."[47] Rupert Schmidt used the photographs for reference in modeling horses that figured in the frieze on the Memorial Arch, "The Progress of Civilization," which was destroyed in the 1906 earthquake. However indirectly, Muybridge's photographs played a part in the memorialization of his former associate.

The catalogue of the Leland Stanford Junior Museum, published by Stanford University Press in 1903, lists the contents of the Museum's galleries. Among the varied contents of the Memorial room, the Muybridge photographs were placed in what seemed to Mrs. Stanford the appropriate context[48] (77).

During the years of his work at the Museum, Peterson became interested in the history of the photographic experiments. Although he found that "for some peculiar reason almost every item of data connected with the Muybridge story seems to have a unique twist to it,"[49] his efforts to straighten out the twists and the responses he received to his inquiries from people who witnessed the work of 1878 and 1879 have helped subsequent researchers in their attempts to untangle the history.

In 1929, the fiftieth anniversary of the Stanford-Muybridge collaboration was celebrated by the board of trustees of the University. In this semi-centennial celebration, the trustees commemorated the "Motion Picture Research conducted by Leland Stanford, 1878–1879, with the assistance of Eadweard J. Muybridge, John D. Isaacs and J. D. B. Stillman."[50] The program ended with the unveiling of two commemorative tablets: one in

Memorial Court, in the central quadrangle of the University; the other, on the site of the Stock Farm, in the vicinity of Muybridge's "motion-picture studio."[51]

In 1962, Gerald Ackerman, professor of art history at Stanford, arranged an exhibition of the Museum's holdings of plates from *Animal Locomotion*. Ten years later, the Stanford Museum produced an exhibition and catalogue of Muybridge's work, *Eadweard Muybridge: The Stanford Years, 1872–1882.*[52] This account of the years of Stanford's and Muybridge's work together reached an audience beyond the Stanford community: the exhibition traveled throughout this country and to cities in Germany, Austria, and Switzerland.

The Stanford-Muybridge history, then, like the experiments that occasioned it, has in the twentieth century come close to making "the rounds of the civilized world," as the *Alta California* put it in the nineteenth. And Muybridge's appreciation of their work together is, by now, generally endorsed. "The circumstances must have been exceptionally felicitous that made co-laborateurs of the man no practical impediment could halt, and of the artist who, to keep pace with the demands of the railroad builder hurried his art to a marvel of perfection that it is fair to believe it would not else have reached in another century."[53]

Anita Ventura Mozley

A Note on the Cesnola Collection of Cypriot Antiquities at Stanford

162 *Early to Middle Bronze Age Cypriot vases.* Center: *red-polished juglet, 2000–1800 B.C.* Left and right: *white-painted juglets, 1800–1650 B.C.* (SM 4492, 762, 3833)

163 *Late Cypriot base-ring ware. Bottle, 1650–1475 B.C. One-handled bowl, 1475–1225 B.C.* (SM 585, 2259)

AT THE TIME OF their purchase from the Metropolitan Museum of Art in 1884, the 5,000 objects of the Cesnola collection in the Leland Stanford Junior Museum consisted of 3,000 vases, 525 lamps, 328 glass objects, 581 terracotta and stone figurines, 390 small bronzes, 41 scarabs, 30 small ivories, 89 amulets, and 16 bronze and silver coins. Despite the damage to the collection caused by the earthquake of 1906, and the subsequent sales of some surviving duplicates, the Stanford Cesnola collection is one of the largest collections of Cypriot antiquities in the United States. It now comprises approximately three thousand objects. (Unfortunately, not all of the surviving Cesnola objects can still be identified. Scarabs, amulets, and coins, for example, were combined with other parts of the Collection after 1906.) The material is described in T.B.L. Webster, "The Cesnola Collection in Stanford," *Opuscula Atheniensia* 8 (1968), pp. 137–148, and also in Paola Villa, "Corpus of Cypriote Antiquities, 1: Early and Middle Bronze Age Pottery of the Cesnola Collection in the Stanford University Museum," *Studies in Mediterranean Archaeology* vol. 20, no. 1 (1969).

A catalogue in Luigi Cesnola's hand in the Museum's archives includes provenances for many objects. Although some may be correct, they are often so imprecise that the collection is largely without archaeological context. The Late Bronze Age artifacts identified by Cesnola as coming from Alambra underscore the problem inasmuch as recent excavations at Alambra sponsored by Cornell University have not discovered any material of this date at the site or in the vicinity. Work conducted on Cyprus since Cesnola's time, however, allows us to place many pieces in their proper historical and artistic framework.

The objects represent cultural sequences from the Early Bronze Age through the Roman period and thus reflect the different artistic influences to which the island was open. Because of its location on the crossroads of the eastern Mediterranean, Cyprus has been both beneficiary and victim of the exchange and the conflict between east and west, north and south throughout its history. Its art reflects these cross-cultural influences, but the artisans of Cyprus were not merely imitators; they often took foreign elements, modified them, and developed their

164 *Late Bronze Age vases from Cyprus.* Left and right: *white-slip jug and tankard, 1650–1475 B.C.* Center: *imported Mycenaean flask, 1225–1050 B.C.* (SM 2495, 2491, 2904)

165 *Base-ring female figurine, Late Cypriot, 1475–1050 B.C.* (SM 475)

166 *Base-ring bull figurine, Late Cypriot, 1225–1050 B.C.* (SM 473)

own, unmistakably Cypriot style. This phenomenon is readily apparent in the Stanford Collection, particularly in the vases of the Bronze Age through the Cypro-Archaic periods (2500–475 B.C.).

The vases exhibit the progression from Early Bronze Age Anatolian types, such as red-polished ware (162, *center*), through the indigenous Cypriot fabrics, in particular the lively decoration of the white-painted ware (162, *left* and *right*) of the Middle Bronze Age and the pleasing base-ring (163) and white-slip wares (164, *left* and *right*) of the Late Bronze Age. Terracotta figurines of this period are also represented; the woman (165) and the bull (166) in base-ring ware are two particularly fine examples. For others, see Roger Davis and T.B.L. Webster, "Cesnola Terracottas in the Stanford University Museum," *Studies in Mediterranean Archaeology* 16 (1964).

In the Late Bronze Age, the Mycenaean Greeks began to exert a strong influence on Cyprus, particularly in the south and east of the island. Contemporary with the indigenous Late Cypriot wares were Mycenaean Greek assemblages, including both imported vases from the Greek mainland (164, *center*) and locally manufactured imitations. Greek cultural and artistic influences upon the island waxed and waned in subsequent periods, but never disappeared.

During the Cypro-Geometric period, native wares such as black-slip ware (167, *left*) continued to be manufactured, as did wares descended from Mycenaean Greek types. Cyprus was ripe, however, for the assimilation of yet other artistic idioms. By the mid-ninth century Phoenicians had settled on the island, bringing with them their own artistic traditions and drawing Cyprus closer to the Levant. The red-slip and black-on-red wares (167, *center* and *right*) introduced to Cyprus by the Phoenicians are well represented in the Stanford Collection.

At the end of the Geometric period and in the succeeding Archaic period, regional artistic styles became more pronounced. Decoration with compass-drawn concentric circles (168), dominated the pottery of the north and west, and an elaborate rectilinear style with geometric and floral motifs (169) dominated that of the south and east. Both styles are abundant in the Stanford Collection. The pictorial compositions of this time, however, are almost completely lacking in the Collection, though a few vases with stylized bird motifs (170) represent this distinctive Cypriot style. Contemporary terracotta figurines include a variety of common Archaic types, male and female votaries and horses with riders (171).

167 *Geometric and Archaic vases from Cyprus.* Left to right: *black-slip jug,* 1050–850 B.C.; *black-on-red bowl,* 750–600 B.C.; *imported Phoenician red-slip oinochoe,* 750–600 B.C. (SM 1125, 4383, 2359)

168 *Bichrome barrel jug of the Cypro-Geometric period,* 850–750 B.C. (SM 2372)

169 *Cypro-Geometric white-painted amphora,* 850–750 B.C. (SM 780)

170 *Bird in black paint, detail of Cypro-Geometric white-painted ware,* 850–750 B.C. (SM 3259)

171 *Cypro-Archaic terracotta figurines.* Center: *votary with tympanum,* 700–475 B.C. Left and right: *horses with riders, second half of the seventh century* B.C. (SM 360, 493, 504)

The Classical period on Cyprus (475–325 B.C.) saw little native innovation in pottery shape and decoration. Though Near Eastern and local expressions continued, the Greek influence prevailed in the pottery industry as well as in other media; imported Greek molds were even employed in the production of terracotta figurines. Classical Greek types are included among the many terracotta figurine heads at Stanford. Many of the small limestone heads show the same influence.

Cypriot art of the Hellenistic (325–50 B.C.) and Roman (50 B.C.–250 A.D.) periods is also represented. The pottery, as well as the terracotta and limestone figurines (172), exhibit the styles of the artistic *koine* of the times. The terracotta lamps are primarily imported Roman types and the Cypriot glass vessels in the collection are blown vases belonging to the Roman period.

The bronzes, like the pottery, represent the Early Bronze Age through the Roman period. They include jewelry, tools, and weapons. Among the most impressive pieces are nine lotus-petaled lampstands discussed by Isabelle K. Raubitschek in "Cypriot Bronze Lampstands in the Cesnola Collection at Stanford," in Ekrem Akurgal, ed., *The Proceedings of the Xth International Congress of Classical Archaeology,* Ankara-Izmir, September 23–30, 1973 (Ankara, 1978), pp. 699–707.

Cypriot studies have been the center of vigorous activity during the past decade. Recent excavations have led to exciting, new discoveries on the island. Special exhibits of Cypriot antiquities have opened on Cyprus itself, in Europe, and in America. The Cypriot antiquities in the Stanford Museum have not been neglected during this renaissance in Cypriot studies. In 1972 they were featured in a special exhibit, for which see Darrell A. Amyx and Isabelle K. Raubitschek, *Antiquities of Cyprus,* exhibition catalogue (Stanford, 1972); and in 1980 an exhibition, still on display, was arranged in the Stanford Museum by Isabelle and Anthony Raubitschek for the Joint Meetings of the American Philological Association and Archaeological Institute of America.

Though modest compared to some of the newer discoveries, the assemblage of Cypriot antiquities at Stanford illustrates most phases of the island's rich history and art, demonstrating the unique role of Cyprus in the history, culture, and art of the eastern Mediterranean.

Mary Lou Zimmerman Munn

172 Hellenistic votary head of a boy, third century B.C. (SM 408)

127

Notes to the Introduction

SA Stanford University Archives
MA Stanford University Museum of Art
    Archives

1 See Benjamin March, *China and Japan in Our Museums* (New York, 1929) for an account of turn-of-the-century holdings in Ann Arbor, Boston, Brunswick, Chicago, Detroit, New Haven, New York, Philadelphia, and Salem.

2 Dated May 7, 1884, Cesnola's letter to Mrs. Stanford on the death of her son was included in Herbert C. Nash, *In Memoriam Leland Stanford Junior* (n.p., n.d.), pp. 186–87: "The sad news moved me profoundly when I recalled the youth's amiability and talents, and the sincere interest he took in our museum. I remember his coming with his tutor to study the collections and the great promise he already gave of becoming some day a fine character and a useful man like his father. I consider his untimely death a great calamity, particularly so because his inclinations were so strong towards my chosen field of labor—the art-training of our American people."

3 September 22, 1883, Leland Stanford Junior Papers, SA.

4 Georges Daressy (1864–1938), then a young Frenchman of nineteen, but later well known as an Egyptologist for his excavations at Medinet Habu and his voluminous writings, taught young Leland how to decipher hieroglyphs.

5 *The Days of a Man: Being Memories of a Naturalist, Teacher and Minor Prophet of Democracy* (New York, 1922), vol. 1: *1851–1899,* p. 123.

6 See the *Sacramento Record Union,* October 4 and 22, 1872, for accounts of Agassiz's visit to Sacramento and the consequences of his dynamic presentation. I am grateful to K. D. Kurutz, curator of education at the Crocker Art Museum for this citation and other information about Agassiz's visit.

7 Undated clipping, presumed to date from 1882, in Stanford Family Scrapbook, D, p. 57. Henry Augustus Ward (1834–1906), the naturalist who formed the collection, had studied with Agassiz and worked in his famous museum in Cambridge. Ward's Scientific Equipment Company was in the business of supplying natural-history cabinets to American colleges from Vassar to the University of Virginia. Ward prepared the natural-history exhibits for both the Philadelphia Centennial in 1876 and the World's Columbian Exposition in 1893, earning the sobriquet "King of Museum Builders." The particular collection bought by Stanford and Crocker included many fossils and also casts of fossils taken from originals in European museums.

8 *Chicago Mail,* April 16, 1887, "The Stanford Museum."

9 April 23, 1892, "A University Museum."

10 Herbert C. Nash, *The Leland Stanford Junior Museum: Origin and Description* (San Francisco, 1886), unpaginated.

11 Luigi P. Cesnola, "Catalogue of the Cesnola Collection," 1884, ms, MA. (The Cypriot antiquities at Stanford are described in a separate note.)

12 For a detailed description, see Roger S. Keyes, "The Van Reed *Surimono* Album," *The Stanford Museum* 3 (1974), pp. 2–12. The gift of Maggie P. Van Reed Biddle of San Jose to the Museum in 1892, the album was one of dozens of objects returned to the University in 1962 in the estate of Pedro J. Lemos, curator of the Museum from 1917 to 1945.

13 "Catalogue of antiquities secured by Mrs. L. Stanford while in Europe in 1888," ms, MA.

14 William Elliot Griffis, *Henry G. Appenzeller, a Modern Pioneer in Korea* (New York, 1912), p. 221. Appenzeller served in Korea from 1885 to 1902.

15 For a scholarly account, see Suzanne Lewis, *Early Coptic Textiles,* exhibition catalogue, Stanford Art Gallery (1969); see also S. Lewis, "A Footnote to the Exhibition of Early Coptic Textiles," *The Committee for Art at Stanford Newsletter,* Summer, 1969.

16 Emil Brugsch, "List of 273 Egyptian objects acquired in Cairo by Jane Lathrop Stanford in January 1901," ms, MA.

17 Emil Brugsch, "List of 35 Egyptian bronzes from the Kyticas collection acquired by Jane Lathrop Stanford in Cairo in 1901," ms, MA.

18 On her first trip to Japan in 1902, Jane Stanford was introduced to Seisuke Ikeda, a prominent art dealer in Tokyo and Kyoto during the last quarter of the nineteenth century. In 1904, she bought a collection of 418 objects from Ikeda's son. "Collection of rare, ancient and modern art of Japan and China, collected by [the] late Mr. S. Ikeda, Kyoto, Japan," ms, MA.

19 *Catalogue of the Anna Lathrop Hewes Collection in the Stanford Museum* (Palo Alto, c. 1903).

20 "Lists of paintings sent to Stanford from Melbourne by T. W. Stanford," ms, MA.

21 I am indebted to professors John H. Thomas and Richard W. Holm of the department of biological sciences at Stanford for this synopsis of the use made of the building over the years by their department.

22 "Annual Report of the Leland Stanford Junior Museum, ending June 30th, 1917," Peterson Papers, SA.

23 "Harry C. Peterson to David Hewes, October 29, 1912," Peterson Papers, SA.

Notes to the Stanford Family Collection

SA Stanford University Archives
MA Stanford University Museum of Art
    Archives

1 For an illuminating essay on Babson and Goodell, see Joseph A. Baird, Jr., "Judge Crocker's 'Art Gallery'," *Crocker Art Museum: Handbook of Paintings* (Sacramento, 1979), pp. 13–17. (The *Handbook* includes a pertinent essay by Richard V. West, "The Crockers and Their Collection: A Brief History.")

2 *California Landscape Painting, 1860–1885: Artists around Keith and Hill,* exhibition catalogue, Stanford Art Gallery (1975), typescript, pp. 8–9.

3 *San Francisco Evening Bulletin,* September 9, 1871, "Art in San Francisco."

4 Ibid.

5 Ibid.; see also September 18, 1871, "Art Items."

6 Nancy Anderson, author of a doctoral dissertation on Bierstadt and the California landscape school, was kind enough to call this inscribed lithograph to my attention.

7 Gordon Hendricks, *Albert Bierstadt: Painter of the American West* (New York, 1973), pp. 224, 261.

8 "An Art Treasure, the Decorations of the Stanford Mansion," undated clipping from the *San Francisco Chronicle,* probably 1876, as recorded in Stanford Family Scrapbook, B, p. 53, SA.

9 Museum records indicate that the two paintings were acquired for Mrs. Stanford by an agent in 1900. The difference in style was probably due to Charles Nahl's collaboration with his half-brother, Hugo Wilhelm Arthur Nahl, as Jeanne Van Norstrand observes in *The First Hundred Years of Painting in California, 1775–1875* (San Francisco, 1980), pp. 38–40, 59.

10 Thomas Hill, *History of the 'Spike Picture' and why it is still in my possession* (San Francisco, n.d.), unpaginated.

11 *Alta California,* "Hill's *Donner Lake,*" November 7, 1875.

12 *The Diaries 1871–1882 of Samuel P. Avery, Art Dealer,* edited by M. F. Beaufort, H. L. Kleinfield, and J. K. Welcher, with a foreword by A. Hyatt Mayor (New York, 1979), opp. p. xxxvii, graph 6.

13 Hill, *History of the 'Spike Picture'.*

14 As late as 1905, Hill was trying to persuade Harry Peterson, curator of the Stanford Museum, to buy *The Last Spike* for the University. An exchange of letters between the two (August 30, 1905, through February 18, 1906) indicates that nothing came of the proposal, though Peterson did his best to raise the funds. The letters are on record in the Biographical Letter Files (Hill-Peterson), California Room, California State Library, Sacramento.

Stanford Family Collection, *continued*

15 The Muybridge holdings at Stanford are divided among the Museum, the University Archives, and the Department of Special Collections, Stanford University Libraries.

16 For a full account, see chapter 4.

17 William Dean Howells, *The Rise of Silas Lapham,* vol. 12, *Selected Edition of the Works of W. D. Howells,* introduction and notes by Walter J. Meserve (Bloomington, Ind., 1971), pp. 35–36.

18 Charles Marvin, *Training the Trotting Horse* (n.p., 1893), p. 128.

19 *Albany Argus,* January 4, 1886.

20 Earl Shinn [Edward Strahan, pseud.], *The Art Treasures of America* (Philadelphia, [1882?]), p. 54.

21 The second was the fateful trip of 1883–84, which ended with the death of Leland Stanford Junior; the third, a long summer in Germany in 1888; the fourth, a season in London, Paris, Vienna, and Florence, in 1890; and the fifth, a summer at Aix-les-Bains in 1892 for Governor Stanford's health. As a widow, Jane Stanford revisited Europe another three times, in 1897, 1899, and on her way around the world in 1900–1901, a tour that included Egypt and the Holy Land. In 1902, she took her first trip to Japan. And in 1903, she spent a year traveling in the Far and Near East, beginning her trip in Australia and ending it in Japan.

22 Jane Stanford to Leland Stanford, November 8, 1880, Berlin, SA.

23 JS to LS, November 14, 1880, Antwerp, SA.

24 JS to LS, March 16, 1881, Naples, in Gunther W. Nagel, *Jane Stanford: Her Life and Letters* (Stanford, 1975), p. 20.

25 *In Memoriam Leland Stanford Junior* (no author, n.p., n.d.), attributed to Nash, ca. 1884, printed copy, SA; and *The Leland Stanford Junior Museum: Origin and Description* (San Francisco, 1886). Also attributed to Nash, *The Leland Stanford Junior Museum* (Stanford, 1903).

26 JS to LS, November 14, 1880, Antwerp, SA.

27 JS to LS, March 24, 1881, Rome, SA. The bronze group was installed in the Museum lobby in 1893, but later removed.

28 JS to LS, March 28, 1881, Rome, in Nagel, *Jane Stanford,* p. 21.

29 *San Francisco Chronicle,* May 14, 1882.

30 Howells, *Silas Lapham,* p. 215.

31 Francis Haskell, *Rediscoveries in Art—Some Aspects of Taste, Fashion and Collecting in England and France,* the Wrightsman Lectures, delivered under the auspices of the New York University Institute of Fine Arts (Ithaca, 1976), pp. 55–56.

32 *San Francisco Chronicle,* May 14, 1882. All subsequent descriptions of the Old Masters are taken from this source unless otherwise noted.

33 Calvin Tomkins, *Merchants and Masterpieces: The Story of the Metropolitan Museum of Art* (New York, 1970), p. 69.

34 Emile Zola, *Salons,* edited by F. W. J. Hemmings and Robert J. Niess (Geneva, 1959).

35 The journal, which was kept from April 17 to August 10, 1881, is among the Leland Stanford Junior Papers, SA.

36 For a detailed account, see Carol M. Osborne, "Stanford Family Portraits by Bonnat, Carolus-Duran, Meissonier, and Other French Artists of the 1880s," *The Stanford Museum* 10–11 (1980–81), pp. 2–12.

37 Quoted in Tomkins, *Merchants and Masterpieces,* p. 56.

38 Nash, *The Leland Stanford Junior Museum,* 1886, unpaginated.

39 Nash, *In Memoriam,* p. 34.

40 Nash, *The Leland Stanford Junior Museum,* 1886, unpaginated.

41 Leland Stanford Junior to Aunt Kate, December 25, 1883, Vienna, SA.

42 JS to LS, March 24, 1881, Rome, SA.

43 Nash, *The Leland Stanford Junior Museum,* 1886, unpaginated.

44 LS to Heinrich Schliemann, Sunday [January (13?), 1884], Athens, from the Schliemann Papers, Gennadius Library, American School of Classical Studies, Athens. A copy of the letter regretting that the family's engagements would not permit them to accept the invitation to go to Marathon the next day was kindly sent to me by Christina Varda, archivist.

45 *Memoirs of Heinrich Schliemann, a Documentary Portrait Drawn from His Autobiographical Writings, Letters, and Excavation Reports* (New York, 1977), p. 3.

46 A letter from Sophia Schliemann to JS, July 4, 1891, Athens, SA, indicates that she dispatched photographs of her late husband to William Couper for use in fabricating the sculpture: "I have sent the best photographs I have to the sculptor in Florence. I am sure the honour you do to my beloved husband can only equal the high esteem in which he held you and your husband." On August 21, 1891, Jane Stanford wrote from Menlo Park to William Couper in Florence requesting an estimate for a marble sculpture of a large seated figure of Professor Schliemann for the side of the Museum steps. "It would have to be heroic in size as the steps are 312 feet in width." (She meant that the entire front side was 312 feet.) On September 9, 1891, Couper replied that it would give him a great deal of pleasure to make such a sculpture, but that he could not undertake such a seated figure, which would be "an eight-feet statue were it standing," for less than $10,000. All these letters, SA.

47 LSJr to Miss Hull, February 11, 1884, Naples, SA. His correspondent was an especially close friend, the young woman whom the Stanfords had brought from San Francisco to spend the winter of 1882 with them in New York.

Notes to the Leland Stanford Junior Museum

SA Stanford University Archives
MA Stanford University Museum of Art Archives

1 Leland Stanford to Luigi Cesnola, May 13, 1884, New York, Metropolitan Museum of Art, Archives.

2 Luigi Cesnola to LS, May 20, 1884, New York, SA.

3 Charles W. Eliot to David Starr Jordan, June 26, 1919, Asticou, Maine, Jordan Papers, SA.

4 David Starr Jordan, *Days of a Man: Being Memories of a Naturalist, Teacher and Minor Prophet of Democracy* (New York, 1922), vol. 1, *1851–1899,* p. 366.

5 Some eleven hundred pieces were totally destroyed in the earthquake; a representative sample of what remains is on view for the public. Still other material has been used since the days of Hazel D. Hansen, professor of classics at Stanford, for study by students in archaeology.

6 Correspondence between the Stanfords and Luigi Cesnola in the archives of both the Stanford Museum and the Metropolitan treats the subject of these arrangements from 1884 to 1904.

7 Manuscript copy, Stanford Museum. I am indebted to Mary Lou Zimmerman Munn for biographical information about Rhousopoulos gathered in Athens during the summer of 1984.

8 Rhousopoulos ms.

9 *San Francisco Call,* March 14, 1919. In a series of articles by Harry C. Peterson on the founding of the University, which appeared in the *Call* more or less daily from January 13 to April 11, 1919, Peterson recorded that Leland Stanford Junior had inaugurated his International Museum on May 2, 1882, and that the future site he chose for it was where the Stanford stable stood across the corner from the San Francisco house, east of the Fairmont Hotel.

10 Herbert C. Nash, *The Leland Stanford Junior Museum: Origin and Description* (San Francisco, 1886), unpaginated.

11 Harry C. Peterson to Jennie Lathrop Watson, March 11, 1932: "The University was practically founded on Leland's collections in the Stanford Museum, and it was always Mrs. Stanford's wish that they should never be touched but always remain as she placed them. She told me repeatedly that on these collections was founded the University: they were the connecting link between Leland Junior and the cornerstone of the University." Peterson Papers, SA.

12 Carol Sheehan, "Haida Argillite Sculpture at the Stanford Museum," *The Stanford Museum* 10–11 (1980–81), pp. 20–27.

13 Roger S. Keyes, "The Van Reed *Surinomo* Album," *The Stanford Museum* 3 (1974), pp. 2–12.

14 Stanford's role in the construction of the San Jose Post Office was pieced together by Jim

129

Milichich, reference specialist in the Jonsson Library of Government Documents at Stanford, from *A History of Public Buildings under the Control of the Treasury Department* (Washington, D.C., 1901).

15 Alfred Frankenstein, *After the Hunt—William Harnett and Other American Still Life Painters, 1870–1900,* rev. ed. (Berkeley and Los Angeles, 1969), p. 133.

16 *San Francisco Call,* March 19, 1919, article by Harry C. Peterson on the history of the Museum.

17 Ida Honoré Grant to Jane Stanford, August 1, 1884, Long Branch, N.J., Jane Stanford Papers, SA.

18 Julia Dent Grant to JS, March 1889, Washington, D.C., Jane Stanford Papers, SA.

19 Frederick D. Grant to JS, September 17, 1890, Vienna, Jane Stanford Papers, SA.

20 Julia Dent Grant to JS, August 8, 1893, Cranstons-on-Hudson, Jane Stanford Papers, SA. The matter is fully discussed in John Y. Simon, ed., *The Personal Memoirs of Julia Dent Grant,* with notes and forward by Simon (New York, 1975), pp. 23–24.

21 Julia Dent Grant to JS, October 16, 1892, New York, Jane Stanford Papers, SA.

22 *The National Academy of Design Exhibition Record, 1861–1900* (1973) indicates that Campbell exhibited a portrait of General Grant at the Academy in 1887.

23 William Couper to JS, August 12, 1890, Florence, Jane Stanford Papers, SA.

24 The sphinxes were ordered by Mrs. Stanford in Florence during the summer of 1890. Couper wrote to Mrs. Stanford on September 23, 1890, to say that he would begin making them at once. On April 6, 1891, he sent her photographs of models for them, requesting $1,500 to facilitate their progress. At the same time he asked if she would like an inscription pertaining to the family in hieroglyphics on the breastplates of the sphinxes; she declined. Jane Stanford Papers, SA.

25 William Couper to JS, May 25, 1891, Florence, Jane Stanford Papers, SA.

26 Larkin Mead to JS, December 26, 1890, Florence, Jane Stanford Papers, SA.

27 William Couper to JS, May 7, 1891, Florence, Jane Stanford Papers, SA.

28 William Couper to JS, November 7, 1891, Florence, Jane Stanford Papers, SA.

29 Larkin Mead to JS, January 6, 1894, Florence, Jane Stanford Papers, SA.

30 JS to Timothy Hopkins, December 5, 1893, Palo Alto, Jane Stanford Papers, SA.

31 Hopkins was the donor of William Keith's large painting *King's River Canyon, 1878,* now at the Oakland Museum. It joined two other Keiths from the Stanford Family Collection: *Upper Kern River,* 1876 (SM 12057), and a painting entitled in 1882 *Mount Diablo,* which may be the work now called *Marin Sunset* (SM 12026). But a fourth painting, *Headwaters of the Merced, 1875,* has never been in the Museum or the family collection according to old records at Stanford, despite reference to its being purchased by Leland Stanford in Eugen Heuhaus, *William Keith: the Man and the Artist* (Berkeley, 1938), p. 19.

32 William Elliot Griffis, *A Modern Pioneer in Korea: The Life Story of Henry G. Appenzeller* (New York, 1912), p. 221. In a letter from H. C. Peterson to Griffis (March 10, 1912, Palo Alto), the curator reported that the Korean collection was one of the very few to have escaped damage in the earthquake. Peterson Papers, SA.

33 The Viticulture Exhibit in the Horticultural Building is described in *Appendix to the Journals of the Senate and Assembly of the Thirty-First Session of the Legislature of the State of California, 1892–94* 2 (Sacramento, 1895), p. 17. This information was kindly provided by Jim Milichich.

34 *Appendix to the Journals,* p. 170.

35 John Daggett to JS, February 11, 1899, Black Bear, California, letter and "List of Indian Curios at Stanford University," MA. For an account of Daggett's experiences, see "Daggett Writes of Humboldt Indians," *Arcata Union,* May 13, 1911.

36 Ford's *Etchings of the Franciscan Missions of California* (New York, 1883) includes twenty-four prints. Oil paintings of the missions were also executed by Ford; several were to be seen in the Mission Inn, Riverside, California, during the 1960s. Biographical information about Ford supplied by his widow is found in the California State Library, Sacramento, California. Accounts of his life also appear in the obituaries of February 28, 1894 (*San Francisco Call*), and March 3, 1894 (*Santa Barbara Weekly Independent*).

37 Described collectively as the Stanford Mission Music, this important collection was "discovered" by Dr. Carelton Sprague Smith, head of the music division of the New York Public Library, on a visit to the Museum in 1937. The present location of the material is unknown. See also Owen de Silva, *Mission Music of California* (Santa Barbara, 1941), pp. 127–28. This information was kindly provided by John A. Emerson, Music Library, University of California, Berkeley.

38 Hewes was born in Lynnfield, Massachusetts, and educated at Phillips Academy, Andover, and, briefly, at Yale in the class of 1852 with William Morris Stewart, later senator from Nevada and a member of Stanford University's first board of trustees. He and Stewart had first come to California in the Gold Rush and, like Stanford, Hewes had begun his career as a storekeeper in Sacramento. He made his fortune leveling San Francisco's streets with a steam shovel in the 1850s. Success followed him most of his life (at the age of ninety-one Hewes saw to the construction of a nineteen-story office building in Los Angeles). Hewes's autobiography is included in *Lt. Joshua Hewes and Some of His Descendants* (New York, 1913), pp. 225–65. Additional information about his life appears in Leo J. Friis, *David Hewes: More Than the Golden Spike* (Santa Ana, 1974).

39 David Hewes to Harry C. Peterson, September 18, 1904, Orange, Peterson Papers, SA.

40 Philip Schaff, *Through Bible Lands* (New York, 1977; reprint of the 1878 edition), p. 64.

41 Brugsch agreed with the majority of his contemporary Egyptologists that Rameses II was the pharaoh of Israel's oppression, his son Menephtah, the pharaoh of the Exodus; and in his *Geschichte Aegypten unter den Pharaonen, nach den Denkmälern* (1877), frequently quoted by Schaff, Brugsch discussed other aspects of Old Testament history.

42 *Catalogue of the Anna Lathrop Hewes Art Collection in the Stanford Museum* (Palo Alto, c. 1903), pp. 9–20, provides the titles of the paintings.

43 From the document, "Catalogue of D. Hewes' Art Collection, San Francisco," signed and witnessed, June 7, 1889, Peterson Papers, SA: "In consideration of love and affection I hereby give to Miss A. M. Lathrop of the City and County of San Francisco ... all the Pictures, Statuary, Ancient Books, Curios and articles of Virtu mentioned and described in the Catalogue thereof ... It is my wish that the said collection should ultimately pass under the control of the Trustees of the Leland Stanford, Jr., University ... to be placed in the Museum thereof."

44 Emil Brugsch Bey to JS, May 8, 1890, Cairo, Jane Stanford Papers, MA.

45 John Russell Young, *Around the World with General Grant* (New York, 1879), p. 240.

46 The manuscript Koran, which is incomplete, has recently been identified and collated by Edward A. Jajko, Middle East bibliographer at the Hoover Institution: portions of a large manuscript of the Koran, of the kind used in large mosques for public recitation; Muhaqqaq script, eleven lines to the page, by an unidentified and unknown scribe; black ink throughout, with the basmalah, cantillation marks, and some long vowel readings (alif) added in red; ends of verses marked by large gilded rosettes; surah titles in richly ornamented and gilded rectangles; section markers in margins also richly ornamented; occasional manuscript marginal notes, in a different and careless hand, referring to pauses in reading, etc; missing all of surahs 1–24, 29–34, 48, 62–65, and 70–114, and portions of others.

47 David Hewes to Harry C. Peterson, September 18, 1904, Orange, Peterson Papers, SA.

48 For a full description, see Suzanne Lewis, *Early Coptic Textiles,* exhibition catalogue, Stanford Art Gallery (1969).

49 JS to Timothy Hopkins, December 5, 1893, Palo Alto, Jane Stanford Papers, SA.

Leland Stanford Junior Museum, *continued*

50 Harry C. Peterson, "My Personal Connection with the Museum," March 1917, a lengthy memo directed to Ray Lyman Wilbur, Wilbur Papers, SA.

51 Harry C. Peterson to David Hewes, March 3, 1902, Palo Alto, Peterson Papers, SA.

52 Harry C. Peterson, "My Personal Connection with the Museum."

53 Frankenstein, *After the Hunt,* p. 156.

54 *American Register* (Paris), October 1881, Stanford Family Scrapbook, SA.

55 Bertha Berner, *Mrs. Leland Stanford, an Intimate Account* (Stanford, 1934), pp. 105–6. Berner became Mrs. Stanford's personal secretary after the death of Leland Stanford Junior.

56 Cooper's biography is provided in the *San Francisco Call,* October 10, 1897, and the *San Jose Herald,* September 11, 1924, as well as in Eugene T. Sawyer, *History of Santa Clara County* (San Jose, 1922).

57 For a full discussion of Stanford's Australian career, see E. Daniel Potts and Annette Potts, "Thomas Welton Stanford (1832–1918) and American-Australian Business and Cultural Relations," *Historical Studies* (University of Melbourne) vol. 17, no. 67 (October 1976), pp. 193–209.

58 F. B. Smith, "Spiritualism in Victoria in the Nineteenth Century," *Journal of Religious History,* 3 (June 1965), pp. 246–60.

59 The *San Francisco Examiner,* September 6, 1905, provides front-page coverage of the subject together with photographs of Notary Ballou, Mahatma Bailey, and Stanford House.

60 *Catalogue of Oil Paintings in the Collection of T. W. Stanford, Esq.* (Melbourne, 1892), MA.

61 Bernard Smith, ed., *Documents on Art and Taste in Australia: The Colonial Period, 1770–1914* (Melbourne, 1975), pp. 245–47, includes an account of Dickinson.

62 In a letter from Melbourne dated January 28, 1910, to Timothy Hopkins, president of the University's board of trustees, Welton Stanford added that he "placed a high value on those pictures for they were works of art … not being a society man, I did not pay for names that money and ignorance so often popularize."

63 T. W. Stanford to W. E. Caldwell, secretary of the board of trustees, Stanford University, January 12, 1911, Melbourne.

64 During the building's construction, 1899–1903, a third architect, Charles Hodges, was on the site. The decoration was not complete unitl 1905, a year before the earthquake destroyed much of the building. The Church was reconstructed during the period 1908–1913, when the Salviati firm returned with new mosaics for the damaged walls. For further information see Paul V. Turner, *The Founders and the Architects: The Design of Stanford University* (Stanford, 1976).

65 For a full description see Gail Stockholm, *Stanford Memorial Church* (Stanford, 1980), which includes twenty color reproductions.

66 Mauricio Camerino to JS, April 4, 1902, Venice, Jane Stanford Papers, SA.

67 Mauricio Camerino to JS, January 12, 1903, Venice, Jane Stanford Papers, SA.

68 To my knowledge, the only other church in the United States to have been decorated by the combined artistry of the Salviati firm and the Lamb studio is the Church of St. Ignatius Loyola on Park Avenue at 84th Street in New York.

69 Nash, *In Memoriam,* p. 27.

70 Mauricio Camerino to Harry Peterson, November 19, 1904, Venice, MA.

71 JS to Mauricio Camerino, March 1, 1902, Palo Alto, Jane Stanford Papers, SA.

72 JS to Mr. Gage, January 2, 1890, Palo Alto, Jane Stanford Papers, SA.

73 JS to Mauricio Camerino, March 20, 1902, Palo Alto, Jane Stanford Papers, SA.

74 Will of Jane Stanford, February 11, 1897, Jane Stanford Papers, SA: "I direct and authorize the said Trustees … to place and safely preserve in the Leland Stanford Junior Museum … all the following articles, which are in my San Francisco home, my home at Palo Alto, and my home in Washington … which I now name and enumerate. Paintings of every kind, copies as well as originals; water colors, etchings, photographs, mosaic pictures, pictures of all kinds, including family portraits; all curios, all antiquities, mosaics of all kinds; vases, clocks, Venetian mirrors and glasses of all kinds; the large orchestrion and its rollers in the art gallery; all musical instruments; all pedestals, articles of virtu; works of art of every description, bronzes of every kind, marbles of every kind; all the library, books, maps, charts, manuscripts; also all the Elkington silver dinner service; all the Russian gold and silver table ornaments and service; gold and silver plate of all descriptions…."

75 See, for example, Kevin Starr, *Americans and the California Dream* (1973; paperback ed., Santa Barbara, 1981), pp. 33–34.

76 Harry C. Peterson, "My Personal Connection with the Museum."

77 Nathaniel Burt, *Palaces for the People* (Boston, 1977), pp. 168–69.

78 Harry C. Peterson, "My Personal Connection."

79 George A. Dorsey to Harry C. Peterson, May 11, 1903, Albuquerque, Peterson Papers, SA.

80 George A. Dorsey to Harry C. Peterson, June 20, 1902, Chicago, Peterson Papers, SA.

81 Quoted in Timothy H. H. Thoresen, "Paying the Piper and Calling the Tune: The Beginnings of Academic Anthropology in California," *Journal of the History of the Behavioral Sciences* vol. 11, no. 3 (July 1975), p. 260. This article and others on Phoebe Hearst were kindly brought to my attention by William Roberts, archivist, University of California at Berkeley.

82 F. W. Putnam, *Guide to the Collections of the Department of Anthropology at the Affiliated Colleges* (San Francisco, 1906), p. 2.

83 Letters and lists from the following agents of the Society in England and the United States account for these gifts: James S. Colton, November 29, 1900, London; Sara Y. Stevenson, December 5, 1901, Philadelphia, and January 11, 1901, Philadelphia; Herbert Lythgoe, August 30, 1905, Boston; Emily Paterson, August 3, 1909, London; and Maria N. Buckman, July 12, 1911, Boston, MA.

84 Copy of JS's contract for the hiring of the "Olga" together with a photograph of the boat, Jane Stanford Papers, SA.

85 Wilbour's description of Chauncey Murch is quoted in John A. Wilson, *Signs and Wonders upon Pharaoh* (Chicago, 1964), p. 112.

86 Berner, *Mrs. Leland Stanford,* p. 145.

87 Chauncey Murch to JS, April 17, 1902, Luxor, Jane Stanford Papers, SA.

88 Emil Brugsch, "Catalogue of Egyptian Antiquities purchased by Mrs. Leland Stanford in Cairo," March 27, 1901, with penciled notation, "Kyticas Collection," MA.

89 Maspero's letter was accompanied by a statement from John G. Long, U.S. consul general, Cairo, authenticating his signature and that of Brugsch, MA.

90 JS to Emil Brugsch, June 1901, Bad Kissingen, Jane Stanford Papers, SA.

91 Emil Brugsch to JS, July 5, 1901, Cairo, Jane Stanford Papers, SA.

92 See "Selective Catalogue of Antiquities Collected by the Stanfords, No. 4, Fragment of a Bronze Offering Table." Ms copy, MA.

93 H.W. Seton-Karr to the president, Leland Stanford Junior University, April 6, 1901, Wimbledon, MA.

94 I am indebted to my Stanford colleagues Priscilla Murray, department of anthropology, and Curtis Runels, program in values, technology, science, and society, for an account of Old World chipped-stone tools in the Stanford Museum from which I have drawn descriptions of this material.

95 R. Rathbun, assistant secretary in charge of the National Museum, Smithsonian Institution, to the president, Leland Stanford Junior University, March 9, 1903, MA.

96 Harry C. Peterson to H. W. Seton-Karr, April 4, 1903, Palo Alto, MA.

97 Harry C. Peterson to H. W. Seton-Karr, July 24, 1908, Palo Alto, MA.

98 H.W. Seton-Karr to Harry C. Peterson, August 28, 1908, Wimbledon, MA.

99 Archibald H. Sayce, *Reminiscences* (London, 1923), p. 434.

100 Emil Brugsch to Harry C. Peterson, May 10, 1903, Cairo, MA.

Leland Stanford Junior Museum, *continued*

101 T. G. H. James, ed., *British Museum: Hieroglyphic Texts from Egyptian Stelae,* pt. 1, 2d ed. (London, 1969), p. 8, no. 2.

102 I am indebted to Patrick J. Maveety, curator of Asian art at the Stanford Museum, for descriptions and accounts of the Ikeda collection.

103 René Brimo, *L'Evolution du goût aux Etats-Unis d'après l'histoire des collections* (Paris, 1934).

104 JS to Mrs. Timothy Hopkins, February 20, 1904, Cairo, Jane Stanford Papers, SA.

105 Ann Douglas, *The Feminization of American Culture* (New York, 1977), p. 226.

Notes to the Architectural Significance of the Stanford Museum

SA Stanford University Archives
MA Stanford University Museum of Art Archives

I acknowledge gratefully the work of the following people who have conducted research on the history of the Stanford Museum: the late J. B. Wells, professor of civil engineering at Stanford; Mrs. Leland King, of the Stanford Committee for Art; and Mary Tussey. Others who have helped me in this study include: Mary Lou Zimmerman Munn, Stanford Museum; Isabelle K. Raubitschek and Jody Maxmin, Stanford art department; Jack Winkler, Stanford classics department; Roxanne Nilan and Linda Long, Stanford University Archives; Grace E. Baker, Society of California Pioneers, San Francisco; and Johan Kooy, archivist, California Academy of Sciences, San Francisco.

1 For a general survey of the history of museum architecture, see Nikolaus Pevsner, *A History of Building Types* (Princeton, 1976), chapter 8. For nineteenth-century museums in Europe, see also B. Deneke and R. Kahsnitz, ed., *Das kunst- und kulturgeschichtliche Museum im 19. Jahrhundert* (Munich, 1977).

2 It should be pointed out that nineteenth-century European museums of natural history constitute a separate category, and used nonclassical styles of architecture more frequently than did the European museums of art. For the nineteenth-century American museums, see Laurence Vail Coleman, *The Museum in America* (Washington, D.C., 1939), vol. 3, pp. 683–89, and *Museum Buildings* (Washington, D.C., 1950), vol. 1, chapter 6; Nathaniel Burt, *Palaces for the People: A Social History of the American Art Museum* (Boston, 1977); and histories of specific museums. The principal art museum buildings in the United States before the Stanford Museum were: Wadsworth Atheneum, Hartford, Connecticut, 1844; Corcoran Gallery, Washington, D.C., 1874; Memorial Hall (Fine Arts Building of Centennial Exhibition), Philadelphia, 1876; Museum of Fine Arts, Boston, original building (now demolished), 1876; Pennsylvania Academy of Fine Arts, Philadelphia, 1876; Metropolitan Museum of Art, New York, original building, 1880; Cincinnati Art Museum, original building, 1881; St. Louis Museum, original building, 1881; Art Institute of Chicago, original building (now demolished), 1885; Detroit Museum of Art, original building, 1888.

3 Pevsner, *Building Types,* pp. 124, 128.

4 J. Mordaunt Crook, *The British Museum* (New York, 1972), p. 88.

5 Among the very few earlier American museums that might be called Neoclassical were the Pilgrim Society Museum, Plymouth, Massachusetts, 1824, and the Trumbull Gallery, Yale University, 1832 (the first museum at an American college or university)—both products of the Greek Revival.

6 Herbert C. Nash, *In Memoriam Leland Stanford Junior* (n.p., n.d.), p. 26. See also Nash's *The Leland Stanford Junior Museum: Origin and Description* (n.p., 1886), a catalogue of the collection when it still was in the Stanfords' San Francisco house.

7 Nash, *In Memoriam,* pp. 23, 26.

8 Ibid., pp. 23ff.

9 David Starr Jordan, *The Days of a Man* (New York, 1922), p. 385. This is the first record of the story that I have found. Jordan was the first president of Stanford University, and could have heard the story from the Stanfords themselves.

10 Αγγελικη Κοκκου, Η ΜΕΡΙΜΝΑ ΓΙΑ ΤΙΣ ΑΡΧΑΙΟΤΗΤΕΣ ΣΤΗΝ ΕΛΛΑΔΑ ΚΑΙ ΤΑ ΠΡΩΤΑ ΜΟΥΣΕΙΑ [Angeliki Kokkou, *Concern for the Antiquities in Greece and the First Museums*] (Athens, 1977), pp. 201–57. See also: Κωστα Μπιρη, ΑΙ ΑΘΗΝΑΙ ΑΤΤΟ ΤΟΥ 19ογ ΕΙΣ ΤΟΝ 20 οη ΑΙΩΝΑ [Kostas Bires, *Athens from the 19th to the 20th Century*] (Athens, 1966), pp. 210ff; Hans Hermann Russack, *Deutsche Bauen in Athen* (Berlin, 1942); and *Thieme-Becker Künstler-Lexikon* (Leipzig, 1907) for entries on Lange and Ziller. Special thanks are due to Angeliki Kokkou for providing us with a copy of her book and for supplying the photographs of the National Museum reproduced in the text.

11 Pevsner, *Building Types,* p. 125; Deneke and Kahsnitz, *Museum im 19. Jahrhundert,* pp. 181–83. Pevsner (pp. 118–21) has traced this plan type back to the eighteenth-century French academic designs, as codified in J. N. L. Durand's publications of c. 1800.

12 *San Francisco Examiner,* April 28, 1887; Shepley, Rutan & Coolidge ledger labeled "H.H.R. &S.R.&C. Receipts, 1885–1889," pp. 137–38 (examined by me in the archives of Shepley, Bulfinch, Richardson & Abbott, Architects, Boston, 1976). There is no known evidence of the design itself, or of its date; but the fact that Shepley, Rutan & Coolidge did produce a design for the Stanford Museum is confirmed in a letter from the firm to John K. Branner, June 30, 1910, Boston, SA.

13 *Stanford University: The Founding Grant* (Stanford, 1971), pp. 3–4; report by Francis A. Walker to Leland Stanford, November 30, 1886, reproduced in Orrin L. Elliott, *Stanford University: The First Twenty-Five Years* (Stanford, 1937), pp. 587–95. Olmsted and Coolidge's principal master plan for the University was published in *Garden and Forest,* December 19, 1888, pp. 507–8. See also Paul V. Turner, Marcia E. Vetrocq, and Karen Weitze, *The Founders and the Architects* (Stanford, 1976), pp. 30–39.

14 *San Francisco News Letter and California Advertiser,* December 24, 1887, p. 42.

15 Henry S. Codman to John Olmsted, October 10, 1889, Palo Alto, Olmsted Papers, Library of Congress; copies in SA.

16 Henry S. Codman to Frederick Law Olmsted, April 21, 1890, Olmsted Papers, Library of Congress; copies in SA.

17 The precise date of this decision is not known. There is a puzzling map in the Stanford Planning Office, dated October 1889, which shows the Museum in its present location; but it is possible that the building was added to the plan later.

18 See my essay "The Collaborative Design of Stanford University," in *The Founders and the Architects.*

19 See my *Campus: An American Planning Tradition* (New York, 1984), chapter 5.

20 Ernst Ziller to JS, August 21, 1888, Athens, MA.

21 Ernst Ziller to JS, September 8, 1888, Athens, MA.

22 Irving J. Manatt to JS, October 1, 1890, Athens, MA.

23 Herbert C. Nash to Percy & Hamilton, October 26, 1890, Percy & Hamilton Scrapbook, Society of California Pioneers, San Francisco.

24 JS to Percy & Hamilton, October 29, 1890, Percy & Hamilton Scrapbook, Society of California Pioneers, San Francisco. The "Photos"—presumably those of the National Museum in Athens sent to Mrs. Stanford in Manatt—are not known to survive.

25 See the biographical entries on Percy and on Hamilton in H. F. and E. R. Withey, *Biographical Dictionary of American Architects* (Los Angeles, 1956, pp. 259–60, 468; and in *The Bay of San Francisco ... A History* (Chicago, 1892), vol. 1, p. 659, and vol. 2, p. 132.

26 Withey, *Bay of San Francisco;* David Gebhard et al., *A Guide to Architecture in San Francisco and Northern California* (Santa Barbara, 1973), pp. 91, 368; Michael R. Corbett, *Splendid Survivors: San Francisco's Downtown Architectural Heritage* (San Francisco, 1979), p. 207.

27 Bertha Berner, *Mrs. Leland Stanford, an Intimate Account* (Stanford, 1934), p. 51.

28 Stanford University Archives does, however, possess a photostatic print of an elevation drawing (undated) of the Museum's façade, which appears to be part of the original design. This is preserved in a collection of architectural documents which also contains prints of drawings for later stages of the Museum's construction.

29 *San Francisco Chronicle,* January 14, 1891, p. 5. One clue that this is not a drawing by the architects themselves is that the pilasters of the central portico are mistakenly shown as freestanding columns, an error that could easily be made by someone not familiar with the design, sketching from an elevation drawing of the façade.

30 Ibid.

31 Among Percy's technical papers was "Practical Applications of Iron and Concrete to Resist Transverse Strains," in *Technical Society of the Pacific Coast: Transactions* 5 (June, 1888), pp. 1–18. I thank Karen Weitze, who brought this article to my attention.

32 Ernest L. Ransome and Alexis Saurbrey, *Reinforced Concrete Buildings* (New York, 1912), pp. 4–5. Construction of the building began in July 1889, and it was occupied in 1891 (information from Johan Kooy, archivist, California Academy of Sciences, San Francisco). The building was demolished following the 1906 San Francisco earthquake and fire.

33 George W. Percy, "Concrete Construction," *The Engineering Record,* March 24, 1894, p. 272.

34 "Architects Inspect the New Concrete Building at Palo Alto," *Oakland Enquirer,* September 28, 1891.

35 The *San Francisco Chronicle,* January 14, 1891, reported that the building was to be of "artificial stone, in order to erect it as speedily as possible," and noted that it was to be "finished and dedicated on the 1st day of next October."

36 Percy, "Concrete Construction," p. 273. For Roble Hall, see also Ransome and Saurbrey, *Reinforced Concrete Buildings,* p. 6, and *The California Architect and Building News* (August 1892), p. 90. The upper floors of Roble Hall were later removed, and now (as Sequoia Hall) the building is only a truncated version of its original form.

37 See Peter Collins, *Concrete: The Vision of a New Architecture* (London, 1959); Carl W. Condit, *American Buildings* (Chicago, 1968), pp. 158–76; and Ada Louise Huxtable, "Concrete Technology: Historical Survey," *Progressive Architecture* (October 1960), pp. 144–49.

38 Berner, *Mrs. Leland Stanford,* p. 58. For the Ponce de Leon Hotel, see Condit, *American Buildings,* p. 159. The city of St. Augustine possessed, in fact, several pioneering concrete structures the Stanfords could have seen in 1888, including two churches with unreinforced concrete walls (see Huxtable, "Concrete Technology," p. 147).

39 For Ransome's career, see Ransome and Saurbrey, "Personal Reminiscence by Ernest L. Ransome," *Reinforced Concrete Buildings,* pp. 1–17, Collins, *Concrete: The Vision,* pp. 61–64; Condit, *American Buildings,* pp. 171–74; Percy, "Concrete Construction"; C. W. Whitney, "Ransome Construction in California," *The Architect and Engineer* (April 1908), pp. 48–52; Ada Louise Huxtable, "Reinforced-Concrete Construction: The Work of Ernest L. Ransome," *Progressive Architecture* (September 1957), pp. 139–42; and Reyner Banham, "Ransome and Bayonne," *Society of Architectural Historians Journal* (December 1983), pp. 383–87.

40 Condit, *American Buildings,* p. 171.

41 United States Patent Office, patent no. 305,226, dated September 15, 1884 ("Building Construction").

42 Condit, *American Buildings,* p. 171; Whitney, "Ransome Construction," p. 48. Collins, *Concrete: The Vision,* p. 62, dates the Alameda factory somewhat later, about 1892.

43 Besides the articles listed below, see "A Notable Concrete Building," *Engineering News,* February 16, 1893, pp. 162–63, and a story in the *Oakland Enquirer,* September 28, 1891, reporting the inspection of the Museum during its construction by a "delegation of fifty members of the Architects' and Technical societies of San Francisco, invited by Messrs. Ransome and Cushing, the contractors of the museum building." In 1938, Professor J. B. Wells of Stanford recorded information about the construction of the Museum provided by Percy Keatinge, whose father worked on the construction and who recalled it himself, MA.

44 *The American Architect and Building News,* 34 (November 7, 1891), p. 84.

45 *The Scientific American,* October 10, 1891, p. 225.

46 *The Engineering Record,* March 24, 1894, pp. 272–73.

47 E.g., these rods (about one inch in diameter), were exposed in 1960 in one of the walls of the Meidel Room, on the second floor of the Museum.

48 United States Patent Office, patent no. 405,800, dated June 25, 1889 ("Finishing Concrete and Artificial-Stone Surfaces").

49 Collins, *Concrete: The Vision,* p. 62.

50 *The Engineering Record,* March 24, 1894, p. 272. I thank Robert Mittelstadt, architect, who examined with me the concrete surface of the Museum.

51 *The Leland Stanford Junior Museum* (Stanford, 1903), p. 3.

52 See *Engineering News,* May 10, 1906, pp. 509–11; *The Founders and the Architects,* pp. 53–57; Gretchen W. Smith and Robert Reitherman, *Damage to Unreinforced Masonry Buildings at Stanford University in the 1906 San Francisco Earthquake* (Redwood City, CA, 1984).

53 See Paul V. Turner, "The Library That Never Was," *Imprint of the Stanford Libraries Associates* (April 1976), pp. 4–13; and *The Founders and the Architects,* pp. 48–51.

54 SA. The specifications state that Charles E. Hodges was to supervise the construction for Percy & Hamilton. A print of an architectural drawing for this stage of the construction survives as well, SA. It is labeled "Percy and Hamilton, Architects," and it shows two sections, cut through a gallery and one of the rotundas, revealing the brick wall and concrete floor construction (with "½-inch twisted rods" specified for the rib beams of the concrete floor slabs). Also see *Engineering News,* May 10, 1906, p. 510.

55 SA.

56 Paoletti's watercolor drawings are preserved in SA.

57 Letters concerning this phase of the construction, from Charles E. Hodges to JS (1901–2), and specifications for the work (1902–4), are in SA, as are prints of twelve drawings by Hodges, of various details of his additions to the Museum. The Stanford Museum itself possesses a print of a large floor plan of the entire building, which probably was drawn during this period (or perhaps even earlier, by Percy & Hamilton, as a master plan).

58 *The Leland Stanford Junior Museum,* p. 3.

59 *Engineering News,* May 10, 1906, p. 510. See also H. F. Stoll, "Durability of Reinforced Concrete," in *Cement Age,* 1 (April 1907), pp. 243–45; Whitney, "Ransome Construction," pp. 48–52; and Smith and Reitherman, *Damage,* pp. 18–19.

60 Stanford University Archives possesses prints of drawings, labeled "A. J. Bain, Architect" and dated April 1909, for remodeling various parts of the Museum for use as classrooms, medical laboratories, etc., and miscellaneous specifications for this work.

Notes to the Stanfords and Photography

SA Stanford University Archives
SC Special Collections, Stanford University Libraries
SM Stanford University Museum of Art

1 Glenn G. Willumson, "Alfred Hart: Photographer of the Transcontinental Railroad," master's thesis, University of California, Davis, 1984.

2 Archibald Treat had worked in Stanford's San Francisco office in the late 1870s and early 1880s. Prints of his "progress reports," SC.

3 Beaumont Newhall, "Photography and the Suspense of Time," the Frederick W. Brehm Memorial Lecture, George Eastman House, Rochester, N.Y., October 22, 1954.

4 Stanford Family Scrapbook, 6, SA.

5 Robert B. Haas, *Muybridge, Man in Motion* (Berkeley and Los Angeles, 1976), p. 46. Hereafter cited as Haas.

6 *London Photographic News,* May 11, 1869. Quoted in Haas, p. 47.

7 Eadweard Muybridge, "Leland Stanford's

Gift to Art and to Science," *San Francisco Examiner,* February 6, 1881. Hereafter cited as Muybridge, "Stanford's Gift." The entire article is quoted in Anita V. Mozley, Robert B. Haas, Françoise Forster-Hahn, *Eadweard Muybridge: The Stanford Years, 1872–1882* (Stanford, 1972), pp. 119–23. The Stanford publication hereafter cited as *Stanford Years.*

8 Haas, p. 82.

9 Advertisement in the scrapbook of clippings about his career that Muybridge compiled. This source of newspaper and other comment on his work is in the collection of the Museum of Kingston-on-Thames, Muybridge's birthplace. Hereafter cited as Kingston Scrapbook.

10 Verso of the illustrated card titled Panorama of San Francisco from the California Street Hill, SA.

11 E. J. Marey, *Animal Mechanism,* vol. 11 of *The International Scientific Series* (London and New York, 1874), pp. 147–48 and 138, quoted in *Stanford Years,* p. 87.

12 Muybridge to Gaston Tissandier, editor of *La Nature,* February 17, 1879. Quoted in full in *Stanford Years,* p. 117.

13 Marey, *Animal Mechanism,* p. 137.

14 Map of the Palo Alto Stock Farm, *Semi-Centennial Celebration in Commemoration of the Motion Picture Research Conducted by Leland Stanford, 1878–79* (Stanford University, 1929), unpaginated, SA.

15 Although the article is unsigned, the language is certainly Muybridge's. In it, Muybridge alludes to the telegraphic connection conceived and executed by David Hewes for the driving of the last spike, when completion of the transcontinental railroad was signaled to both coasts.

16 This and the following quotation from *Pacific Rural Press,* June 22, 1878, from Haas, p. 110.

17 Tissandier published Marey's results in *La Nature* on September 28 and October 5; Muybridge's on December 14, 1878.

18 Translated in *Stanford Years,* p. 116.

19 Frank Shay, *A Lifetime in California,* chapter 43, p. 3, ms, SA.

20 "Now he [Stanford] bade the artist to put the pictures themselves in motion. Again the artist urged that science had found no way of doing such a thing. It was of no avail, and for two years and a half the railroad builder and the photographer toiled with a child's toy—the zoötrope—as the initial point, and finally emerged with the zoögyroscope, signifying generally animals in motion." Muybridge, "Stanford's Gift."

21 Muybridge, "Stanford's Gift."

22 Muybridge, Preface to *Animals in Motion* (London, 1899), p. 14.

23 Muybridge, "Stanford's Gift."

24 Haas, p. 46.

25 In his Preface to *Animals in Motion,* 1899, Muybridge remarks: "With the exception of a series of phases of a solar eclipse, made in January, 1880, the Palo Alto researches were concluded in 1879." By this time dry gelatin-bromide photographic plates were replacing wet-collodion.

26 Copy in SC.

27 Meissonier's biographer reports that the painter had even had a railroad constructed around a running track, so he could move at the speed of running horses and thus observe their movements more accurately. Vallery K. O. Gréard, *Meissonier: His Life and His Art* (London, 1897), vol. I, p. 78. The article, signed VAL, is dated "Paris, June 26, 1881." It is titled, in the spirit of those times, "How Governor Stanford Converted Meissonier. The Great Horse Painter Finds that He Has Been in Error as to the Horse all His Life."

28 *Le Globe,* Paris, September 27, 1881, from the Kingston Scrapbook, quoted in Haas, p. 130.

29 *American Register,* Paris, December 3, 1881. From the Kingston Scrapbook, quoted in *Stanford Years,* p. 85.

30 Eadweard Muybridge to Frank Shay, November 28, 1881, Paris; Bancroft Library, University of California, Berkeley.

31 Eadweard Muybridge to Frank Shay, December 31, 1881, Paris; Bancroft Library, University of California, Berkeley.

32 James R. Osgood & Co. to Dr. J. D. B. Stillman, December 30, 1881, Boston, SA.

33 Unidentified journal, Kingston Scrapbook, quoted in Haas, p. 132.

34 *Photographic News,* London, March 17, 1882, from the Kingston Scrapbook.

35 *San Francisco Morning Call,* April 9, 1882, from the Kingston Scrapbook, quoted in full in Haas, pp. 133–34.

36 *Illustrated London News,* March 28, 1882, from the Kingston Scrapbook.

37 Eadweard Muybridge to Dr. J. D. B. Stillman, March 7, 1881, London, SA. Quoted in full in *Stanford Years,* p. 125.

38 Transcript of a copy of the original record of *Muybridge vs. Osgood,* SA.

39 Dr. J. D. B. Stillman to James R. Osgood & Co., April 10, 1882, San Bernardino, SA. Muybridge realized his ambition of producing a work comparable to Audubon's when the University of Pennsylvania published his *Animal Locomotion* in 1887.

40 Leland Stanford to Dr. J. D. B. Stillman, October 23, 1882, New York, SA.

41 LS to Dr. J. D. B. Stillman, January 5, 1883, New York, SA.

42 Eadweard Muybridge to LS, draft version, May 2, 1892, San Francisco. In it, Muybridge also mentions Mrs. Stanford's "desire to extend the

investigation" beyond the summer of 1878. Muybridge was in San Francisco in 1892 preparing for a zoöpraxigraphical tour of the Far East. Instead, he took his zoöpraxiscope to the World's Columbian Exposition in Chicago.

43 William R. French to LS, April 7, 1883, Washington, D.C., enclosing "The Horse in Motion, Notes and Criticisms by Wm. R. French, Nov. 1882," SA.

44 James R. Osgood & Co. to Dr. J. D. B. Stillman, February 28, March 8, and June 26, 1882, Boston, SA.

45 James R. Osgood & Co. to Dr. J. D. B. Stillman, January 4, 1883, Boston, SA.

46 LS to Dr. J. D. B. Stillman, January 5, 1883, New York, SA.

47 Peterson papers, SA.

48 *Leland Stanford Junior Museum* (Stanford, 1903).

49 Peterson to R. P. Schwerin, June 6, 1916.

50 Quoted from the title page of the program, SA. Isaacs, who helped make the electrical circuit, did have a part in the experiments, but Stillman deserved no credit for the success of the photographs. As Muybridge said in the draft of a letter to Stanford, May 2, 1892, Stillman "never was present at an experiment in motion."

51 *Semi-Centennial* program.

52 Published by the Department of Art, Stanford University, as Stanford Art Book 14, 1972, 1973. German edition (Stuttgart, 1976).

53 Muybridge, "Stanford's Gift."

Index

136

Credits

Photographs not in the Stanford Museum Collection reproduced
courtesy of Boston, Museum of Fine Arts, 3; Angeliki Kokkou, 129–
131, 133; New-York Historical Society, 35; New York Metropolitan
Museum of Art, 2, 128; Munich Stadtmuseum, 127; Oakland
Museum, 22, 33; Sacramento, California Railroad Museum, 38;
Sacramento, California State Library, 91; Stanford University
Archives, 1, 17, 27, 36, 50, 52, 82, 90, 106, 119, 139, 144; Paul Turner,
135, 141; University of California, Berkeley, Bancroft Library, 147.

Type set by Frank's Type, Mountain View, California
Printed by T. & J. Graphic Arts, Redwood City, California
Bound by Cardoza-James, San Francisco, California

Design: Ann Rosener